T0313278

"Tim Lewko and Thinking Dimensions Global were brought on board because we needed a common approach to strategy that was practical, decision based and integrated financials. In addition, rather than name brand consultants we wanted a strategy process that forced our executives to sweat through tradeoffs and own implementation. Tim's book-Making Big Decisions Better shares the approach we embedded in our business units to drive better performance."

F. Nicholas (Nick) Grasberger, *President and Chief Executive Officer at Harsco Corporation (NYSE:HSC)*

"**Tim Lewko is a straight talking thought leader on the power of effective strategic planning**. This book provides **a formula for taking strategic planning out of the retreat format** and establishing it as the foundation for business success. This is hard work, but it's easier than turning around a failing business."

Gordon Clemons, *Chairman of the Board, CEO and President at CORVEL ORP (NASDAQ:CRVL)*

"**An outstanding book, with absolute simplicity** gives the needed support for driving focused business decisions. Being an entrepreneur in a family generational business in Veneto, Italy – I appreciate the genuine approach it offers. **A true value difficult to find nowadays**."

Paulo Moresco, *Managing Director and CEO, 3M Holding, Veneto, Italy, a company with a global investment portfolio*

"How many strategy books have you read and then thought, '**Great, how do I start?**' *Making Big Decisions Better* **is in fact the step by step menu needed to make real change in your organization**. Mr. Lewko's simple 'Fix. Build. Use.' outline walks you through both the Why and the How of strategy development."

John Case, *President, Consumer Products Group, Leggett & Platt*

"In *Making Big Decisions Better*, Tim gives both practicing and would-be strategists a **simple how-to guide to create a strategy that delivers improved EBITDA to any organization**. This book does not describe an esoteric or academic approach to strategy; it a **road map to successful strategy formulation and implementation obviously written by someone whose how been in the trenches doing it**. Great read for anyone wanting to create a winning strategy and implementation plan."

Roger Miller, *Chief Executive Group Chair at Vistage International*

"To develop effective strategy for a global organization is hard work. **The strategy process developed by the author in *Making Big Decisions Better* works!** We engaged the author to help us significantly re-orient our global trade organization, a complex task, and the result was very positive for our customers."

John Holland, *former President of the International Copper Association*

"I have worked with Tim on a number of occasions in the past and am not surprised that he can so easily communicate effective ideas and tools to help move a business forward. Sustainable success can be achieved through simple targeted strategy that can easily be communicated to an organization. **This book is genuine, and will most certainly help you achieve greater results professionally**."

Scott C. Ride, *Chief Operating Officer, The Hillman Group, Canada*

"My immediate reaction to this book, these ideas and these philosophies is—**practical, accessible and useful**. I read a lot of business books, most of them are a little on the airy side, but this one resonates. **It's incredibly authentic. The ideas will have an immediate impact on your business**. A rarity these days."

Amy Cosper, *former Editor-in-Chief, Entrepreneur Magazine, Founder, RadicalUpstarts*

"**Having subscribed to the methodology illustrated in the book**; successfully defining, executing and achieving **strategy becomes much more clear and attainable**. Strategy moves from opaque to transparent, as well as easily communicated throughout the company."

Daniel J. Starck, *Chief Executive Officer and Director, Apria Healthcare Group Inc.*

"I admit, I am the CEO of a client company. I met the CEO of another client company many years ago at 37.000 ft. somewhere over the Atlantic on my commute home to the US. We discussed my challenge, **how to change the culture of the business to which I had recently been appointed CEO, how to accelerate the pace of developments and how to accelerate growth**. This book captures the substance of that conversation, the concepts that galvanized me to act and embrace the lessons that you will find in these pages. **An easy read with practical, no nonsense processes that can transform your company**."

Steve Cassidy, *President and CEO, Selig Sealing Products Inc.*

"**Practical, specific and effective**. Each chapter made me think about my path. On one hand it confirms that I am moving in the right strategic direction. I think about the techniques I have already adopted to deliver business results: team involvement, P&L training, a shared strategy. On the other hand, **this book provided new and usable decision making tools to make more efficient business choices every day**."

Maurizio Bazzo, *President and CEO of INglass S.p.A; 2015 Italian Ernst & Young Entrepreneur of the Year award, Industrial Products category*

"**After endless theoretical strategy books, it is really rewarding to get stuck into some ideas for doing**. The book presents **a practical toolkit for driving a business to success** through an **increasingly complex environment**. Approaches to unravelling often overlooked areas such as strategic latitude are superbly explained and applied."

James Allsop, *Area General Manager, Bard UK Limited*

"Tim Lewko's consulting expertise is **practically oriented and directed at leaving the company with tools with which it can help itself to grow the bottom line year on year**. He has a practical approach and gets to the core of the issues very quickly. The distillate of his work is always a series of concise actions that can be implemented by the management team to grow the business and its cash flows. The book contains much of Tim's decades of experiences and many of these tools. It is highly recommended to anyone engaged in the practice of strategy. Also, it is much cheaper than hiring him directly."

Andrew Warrington, *President, United Conveyor Corporation*

"Charles Kepner showed us the importance of rational process in directing our thinking. Daniel Kahneman showed us that our brain's System 1 thinking circuits all too often keep us from utilizing those fundamental processes. As a consequence, and particularly in the area of strategy, we find ourselves confronting needless thinking errors based on what we allowed ourselves to assume, expect, believe, or anticipate without having directed a single relevant question to our colleagues or subordinates to verify our thinking. **Tim Lewko is one of the very few practitioners who understands what it takes to overcome our brain's System 1 tendencies and achieve the benefits of rational process. Fortunately for all of us, he has taken the time to make his unique way of thinking visible to all of us in this important book.**"

Al H. Ringleb, *President and Founder,*
CIMBA Italy, CIMBA, Kansas State University

"Tim has helped me and my team to focus our strategic planning on what's really critical and can be implemented. His clear strategic thinking and process are both powerful and simple, and that's the secret to a successful strategy. Most books on strategy are heavy on theory, but Tim's gives you the tools you need to successfully develop and implement a solid business strategy. A very refreshing and effective approach to the topic."

Pablo Toledo, *Acelity General Manager, Brazil*

Making Big Decisions Better

For many organizations, the word strategy conjures up endless ideas, concepts and tools – while the intent is correct, the awful reality is most companies do not have a simple, common definition of strategy or a simple approach to make the big decisions. Too many PowerPoints, not enough one-pagers that can be put into practice. The lack of a common approach to strategy frustrates executives, creates conflict where there is none, fast tracks dubious alternatives, lengthens decision-making and hampers the quality of the decisions that finally emerge. With the pace of change and mountain of data that inundates CEOs and executive teams daily, now more than ever, leaders need to simplify and have a common approach to making decisions that concern the purpose and path of their organization. Strategic thinking cannot be outsourced.

Tim Lewko's *Making Big Decisions Better* explains the bare-bones elements that must underpin strategic decision-making in a practical framework that C-Suite leaders can actually use. Drawing on practical models, stories and client examples, he explains the problem succinctly, offers proven ways forward and provides specific actions to revive strategic thinking, declutter the strategy process and drive better financial outcomes.

This is essential reading for managers, business leaders and anyone interested in a framework for decision-making that is thorough, adaptable and highly practical.

Tim Lewko is the CEO of Thinking Dimension Global consultancy. He works with CEOs and boards on their big decisions – those that involve product, market and future capability choices. His passion lies in forging strong and lasting senior-level relationships with CEOs that enable them to define the purpose and path of their company and realize sustainable EBITDA results.

He has worked with CEOs and Senior Executives using a process versus prescription approach to strategy over the last 17 years across North America, South America, Europe, Asia and India. His clients to date have achieved over 600 million USD in improved EBITDA performance through his advisement and the tools presented in this book.

Making Big Decisions Better

How to Set and Simplify Business Strategy

Tim Lewko

Routledge
Taylor & Francis Group

LONDON AND NEW YORK

First published 2017
by Routledge
2 Park Square, Milton Park, Abingdon, Oxon OX14 4RN

and by Routledge
711 Third Avenue, New York, NY 10017

Routledge is an imprint of the Taylor & Francis Group, an informa business

© 2017 Tim Lewko

British Library Cataloguing-in-Publication Data
A catalogue record for this book is available from the British Library

Library of Congress Cataloging-in-Publication Data
A catalog record for this book has been requested

ISBN: 978-1-4724-5108-8 (hbk)
ISBN: 978-1-315-59323-4 (ebk)

Typeset in Bembo
by Apex CoVantage, LLC

Intent and dedication of this book

This book is for the doers, practitioners, decision makers and leaders of business. It is not theoretical; it is not consulting speak – it is for those who are leaders now, want to be leaders and want to equip those around them to understand and use strategy to make enduring profits for their business.

With escalating speed of change, short attention spans, a wide range of stated and unstated stakeholder needs, and insatiable urge to react rather than thoughtfully respond, we must equip ourselves and our organizations with practical strategy tools that enable ownership, promote more visual decision-making and get back to the basics of finding root cause in performance gaps.

In addition, this book was written for my current clients as a personal and transportable reference to share with their teams as they continue to refine and implement their BIG DECISIONS.

Importantly, I want to thank the CEOs, C-Suite executives and managers who I have had the privilege of being able to work alongside with and advise on making big decisions better. Over the last 17 years, seeing the decision "insides" of over 100 companies and being party to what works and what does not when it comes to strategy was and is the greatest learning experience ever.

Finally a special hug to my wife LA and kids – Sarah, Giorgio and Tommy – for putting up with a 40-week-a-year traveling husband, early mornings and long nights that enabled me to make my thinking visible, do something I love and share what I believe is **truly the simplest way to positively impact the most people in the shortest time possible – strategy**.

Contents

PART III
USE: how to use your strategy to drive results 73

Figures

Tables

Preface

I wrote this book for executive practitioners. Those leaders who want quantified EBITDA and ROIC impact to their business and want a proven way to achieve this.

This book is based on 17 years (and counting) of consulting experience and quantified client success measured in earnings before interest, tax, depreciation and amortization (better known as EBITDA), working across four continents, countless industries, in every type of company from family owned to Fortune 1000, with revenue size of less than 10 million to over 2 billion.

My **PROCESS** approach or system to strategy (i.e., teach others to fish) rather than **PRESCRIPTIVE** approach (i.e., fish for them) makes these tools enduring and real for any CEO, in any company, in any industry who wants to engage those minds and empower their employees to make better strategic decisions.

This book shares authentic gaps in strategy and the corresponding tools my clients use in resolving their strategic issues and achieving better growth and profitability. It also contains examples of company situations to provide context and color.

Introduction

The most important role a CEO arguably owns is setting and executing strategy to realize sustainable and repeatable EBITDA. Money that can be reinvested into the business. Strategy can be made really simple or breathtakingly complex. The overwhelming majority of successful CEOs and leaders I have worked alongside and advised vote for SIMPLE.

The era of 100-page PowerPoint point decks that no one really uses or understands to explain a company's strategy is over.

Why?

This version of strategy as a eureka moment captured in an encyclopedia of insight during a retreat to be fed to employees is not practical. The reality of seeing strategy decks or binders sitting on a shelf tells the story that these formats are seldom if ever used to drive day-to-day decision-making of the company. Ask almost any CEO and they will likely echo those sentiments.

Today few leaders really care to interpret bubble charts, sit through regurgitated quarterly reviews or recite values tracking across their screensavers. These overly complex or feel-good actions miss the mark on what strategy is.

The best CEOs I have seen in action and worked with know their mandate is to chart and execute a course that their leadership team owns, understands and can translate to the employees on the frontlines. It must drive decision-making.

Complexity, abstract concepts or elitism in strategy are not helpful to drive sustainable and predictable decisions and profit.

So let's simplify strategy.

Strategy is decision-making. Decision-making is strategy. The two of them cannot be disconnected. They are in fact the same. Decisions are the currency of business that creates change, makes things happen and propels a company forward.

Leaders make key decisions that impact the hundreds or thousands they manage. There are no bigger decisions than those critical few that define the essence of strategy: **Products, Markets and Capabilities** relative to the competition through the eyes of the customer.

This book on strategy was written for three reasons that emerged and still emerge from my work with clients. Strategy by and large in many, many organizations is:

1   *Misunderstood*

Strategy and strategic thinking as a competency – despite all that has and will be written – is still not practiced or embedded in companies as an approachable and pragmatic tool to test, exploit and mitigate profitability gaps and empower those closest to the frontlines.

Many leaders in companies climb the ladder of responsibility through an operational lens and set of competencies. When they get to own a P&L or become the CEO, in many cases they are "rusty" at strategy or have never even been given a set of tools to set strategy.

They are in no better position to either develop strategy or build this competency with the people around them. Strategy remains elusive and misunderstood. The cycle repeats itself and the company stalls or begins to accept average EBITDA as the norm, as no leaders eliminate the reliance on operational rather than strategic decision-making. This cycle must be lessened or stopped.

2   *Complex*

Strategy tools, methods and lingo have gotten too complex, unapproachable or disjointed from its true purpose. When strategy was "formalized" as a planning approach in the 1950s, it was the birth of a needed management tool and discipline of thinking.

Today I routinely observe a company's strategy residing as a morphed beast of reports, slides, tools, charts and presentations – rather than the critical few set of decisions around Products, Markets and Capabilities.

The misunderstanding of what strategy is abetted by the misdirected need to make it complex makes the administration of the "Strategy Process" more important that the decision-making itself.

The best example of this unneeded complexity is when companies interpret long-range planning, budgeting and strategy development as stand-alone activities! This complexity needs to be removed and strategy put back to where it belongs – as a discipline of decision-making.

3   *Static*

Companies that are successful and deliver enduring profits in the marketplace have a couple of things in common, from my vantage point.

They see **strategy as a dynamic tool** that allows them to make conscious choices and mid-course corrections as influenced by their external environment (e.g., Customers, Regulatory Competition, Technology).

Second, they clearly know WHY they are making tradeoffs and tough choices on a daily basis. Many companies' strategies and strategy processes have become so static or event driven that the word "strategy" brings a roll to the eyes of executives. They cannot wait to complete the retreat so they can get back to the real work of running the business.

Strategy needs to be **reintroduced as tools for decision-making** that create agility, are not event driven and draw on profound competitive insights from the organization to serve its customer better, relative to the competition.

The result?

Greater, more predictable and enduring profitability for those companies that choose this path.

Two sign posts to get more and quickly use information and guidance you want from this book

Each chapter has two components to enable you to quickly scan and reference the critical pieces:

1   After 5pm (at the start of each chapter)

 After 5pm

This box is at the START of every chapter.
It distills the essence and intent of what is being covered.
You can quickly evaluate the chapter and move on if it's not what you are looking for at the moment or dive in for more information.
This "After 5pm" box came about after long sessions with CEOs and their leadership teams – when CEOs would turn at the end of the day and ask me, "What is the concept in a nutshell?"

2   Now what (at the end of each chapter)

 Now what

This short box is at the END of every chapter.

It crystallizes the main points into specific actions that CEOs can consider individually or deploy with their teams immediately.

This box arose from discussions with CEOs who said, "Consulting speak aside – I get it but how can we use it today or apply it now?"

Part I

FIX

The problems limiting strategy

1 The absence of shared language

Why no one is on the same page

 After 5pm

Right now in your organization, strategy has many meanings. Multiple definitions for the same word create confusion and diffusion of focus.

You need to define for your company what strategy is to remove the unseen communication gaps and disconnects that undermine your organization's focus and effectiveness when dealing with issues.

Defining it creates focus. Not defining strategy creates chaos. Only you have the power to make the simple change in your company or area you lead.

What is *your definition* of strategy?

Have you ever been asked that question by your peers or a direct report? Has anyone ever raised their hand during a CEO town hall meeting and said, **"Excuse me Mr. CEO, but what do you mean by strategy?"**

Probably not.

And "Who cares anyway?" you might be thinking.

If you want to **drive speed and profitability** in your organization through better decision-making, you must start by defining what strategy is for your organization.

Today, walking the halls of your organization, each person has their own working definition of strategy. Whether they have read the latest strategy book, adopted something from experience or learned it in their MBA program, everyone has **their definition** but not a common one for the company. And this lack of a standard approach is a major cause of seen and unseen confusion in many companies.

Why? Because when they use the word "strategy," they are not talking about the same thing and no one wants to admit it.

For the last 17 years, I start every new consulting engagement by asking the CEO and executive team within the first five minutes to collectively do ONE thing: take five minutes and answer the following question (see Figure 1.1) and post your answer on the wall. Make sure it is visible.

In most cases, those involved confidently stride to the wall and post their definition of strategy then gaze at their peers' responses, and the room usually goes silent.

If you're playing along now and wondering what happens with this exercise – here are some real responses from a recent manufacturing client executive team who collectively manage and lead over 1000 people across two continents.

> ### What is your definition of strategy?

Figure 1.1 What is your definition of strategy? (Side note: The question is NOT "What is your strategy?" but rather "What is strategy?"; what do you mean when you use the word in your organization and what do employees understand by it? Keep in mind, **these are experienced, seasoned, educated and well-intentioned executives** who are wondering why they have to answer this question for a consultant they have just met but are genuinely intrigued by the answer they themselves will come up with, along with the response of their peers. They hold the power to infuse clarity or misunderstanding in their organizations.)

Real executive responses:

1 Sue: Path to the goal of making money
2 Bob: A way to conquer problems
3 Bill: Tools required to successfully grow the company
4 Peter: A method of thinking to meet a goal
5 John: Work at making a plan to meet the end goals
6 Rick: A plan setting goals
7 Dan: Series of steps required to get to your goal
8 Sam: Commonly understood direction and goals
9 Sara: Style in doing assigned tasks
10 Reg: Plan to grow business and increase revenue
11 Mark: Using appropriate tools to obtain goals
12 Sid: Plan for future actions
13 Paul: The goals and direction a company will create
14 Mike: What direction to improve and grow
15 Sid: How to make more money than the competition

These well-oiled, high-performing leadership team members all have different answers. When I ask them, "What's the So What?" they consistently share the following concerns or comments when comparing responses:

A There are **SIMILARITIES and DIFFERENCES**
B Some talk more about the **WHAT**
C Some talk about the **HOW**
D Some define it as an **END POINT**
E Others see it as a **SET of STEPS or TASKS**
F Some view it as **TOOLS**
G Some see it as **THINKING**
H Many bring up **GOALS or OUTCOMES**
I Some see it as **PROBLEM-SOLVING and DECISIONS**

So at the same time they are all RIGHT and WRONG. One thing is certain: when people in the organization use the word strategy in their meetings, client proposals, customer service hotlines, purchasing department parameters, procurement negotiations and board meetings, they are NOT on the same page.

The complete list, from A to I, is full of potential for misunderstanding, conflict and confusion – all of which is readily avoidable. Yes, there are themes that align, but there is, nevertheless, too much room for ambiguity and uncertainty.

The most powerful observation that hits home for an executive team that has just completed this exercise always comes back to things they can fix to get people on the same page, including:

A **DIFFUSION:**
When we use the word strategy in our day-to-day meetings and conversations, WE ARE PROBABLY TALKING ABOUT DIFFERENT THINGS.

B **UNNEEDED CONFLICT:**
The SOURCE for conflict in our strategy discussions is not usually because of the content but because we are talking about DIFFERENT THINGS at DIFFERENT TIMES.

C **TIME:**
We could SAVE TIME and channel efforts and resources FASTER and more effectively if we had a COMMON DEFINITION.

D **STRATEGIC THINKING:**
Many of us default to operational thinking and talking, even when we are thinking strategically. We need to be aware and improve this part of our thinking and COMPETENCY in our company.

E **GUIDANCE:**
If we are not on the SAME page for what STRATEGY is, what about the 986 people who report to us? How clear are they on what strategy is and how much guidance does our strategy and strategy process really give those on the frontlines making daily decisions?

What to do?

The best CEOs and organizations I have worked with come to the realization that they must define what strategy is for their organization rather than leave it to chance.

This is not about imposing or legislating a RIGHT definition, but rather having a common language and approach for your company that pays immediate dividends.

With respect to all that has been and will ever be written on strategy and the tools to create it, strategy is simply and practically defined as shown in Figure 1.2.

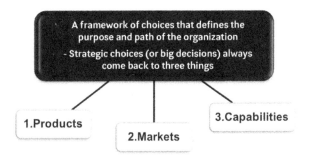

Figure 1.2 Definition of strategy and what the big decisions to be made are

This definition returns everyone back to the simplicity of strategy

Namely, this definition returns everyone to making decisions with data about what products to offer, what markets to serve, and what capabilities to build through the eyes of the customer and relative to the competition. A successful strategy delivers superior profitability or return on invested capital (ROIC) relative to your rivals.

By taking the initiative to define strategy in your organization, you will come away with three powerful benefits immediately available to your organization:

1   **You SIMPLIFY** what should be focused on and with your control: Products, Market and Capabilities relative to the competition.
2   **You ALIGN** the executive team so they are working from the same page of issues and buckets of concerns to deliver on the purpose and path they set for the company.
3   **You BUILD** strategic competencies by having a singular starting point which serves to deepen bench strength of the leadership team and those below them.

 Now what

The absence of a shared language for strategy needs to be resolved simply and quickly. You need to take the simple cost-free step and define it for everyone in your organization.

   Actions to remove the "no one is on the SAME PAGE Gap":

1   **Gather your leadership team**
2   **Have them write and post THEIR definition of strategy**
3   **Choose one definition that becomes the standard definition for your company**

2 Mistaken identity

Strategy is a decision-making process,
not an event

 After 5pm

Many companies don't have a common process to set strategy, nor do they see it as something that should guide daily decision-making of employees. Instead they have getaways or retreats, which provide a false reality that the company is doing and using strategy. This lack of process handcuffs financial performance. One-time events never capture what strategy is.

Unless your industry is static or unchanging, you must have a common strategy process that is used to respond to decisions and outcomes your strategy generates.

Strategy must be engrained as a decision-making tool. Not a meeting.

One of my biggest surprises came from a group of CEOs I was speaking to in New York when I asked this question:

How do you create your company's strategy?

The overwhelming responses were:

- Annual retreat
- Don't have one – too busy with the business
- Don't know
- We use SWOT or Porter's Five Forces
- What do you mean by the question?
- We have tactics already
- Comes from the budget work we do

When asked how that event is used to connect this to daily, functional and individual decision-making, the short answer was: it really didn't.

An event rather than process approach to strategy (see Figure 2.1) **undermines the potential of many companies** in five ways.

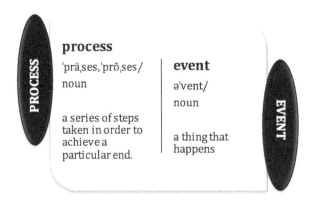

Figure 2.1 Defining process versus event

1   *You assume strategy does not change during the year*

A single event set to the cadence of a calendar year calls into question the dynamism of the industries within which we work. While formal meetings for strategy are needed to gather the minds and data to create it, without these decision points being visible, connected and understood across the organization, you will achieve little change or ownership after the meeting.

Having a process to set and test strategy over the year ensures that you can test what's working and put your finger on the specific areas that aren't.

2   *You reinforce the notion that* **strategy is an abstract concept**

We have all progressed up from lower level positions and at one time or another been sent the email or heard through the grapevine that the "leadership is having an OFF-SITE meeting."

This usually triggers two thoughts from those who aren't attending and, depending on the performance of the company, it's either:

a: **FEAR** – for what impact or changes it might have on my job or
b: **INDIFFERENCE** – I sure hope they listen to us because nothing ever seems to change from those meetings.

These types of responses reinforce the apathy that strategy is unclear, abstract and unknowable. Rather than sharing the process, major issues and expectations for strategy meetings with the entire company – which would serve to engage and groom the employees – people are left to their own imagination and wonderment.

Leadership that lets people guess has limited endurance.

3   *You create the impression that* **only the top people have answers**

When you only have these special events or retreats in boondoggle-worthy places, it serves to underscore to many in the company that strategy is for the "top brass," who create all the answers and then return to disseminate the words of wisdom.

In fact, the best CEOs know that for a strategy to work, you need to invite the right people, those with the right data, insights and expertise – the people who will influence how the company will translate and implement the strategy.

4 *You* under develop *strategic thinking and thinkers*

Having an event mentality and not sharing or making visible the process for strategy undermines the development and competency building of leaders in the organization.

For the larger part of a year, everyone wears their operational hat and, now with these events, both the people attending and those who they report to are left to ponder rather than build the acumen of strategy in their tool kits.

5 *You* remove strategy as a tool *to guide daily decision-making*

Events, as noted at the start, are one-time things that happen. Unfortunately having an event versus a process approach removes the connection and link that strategy is a decision-making tool and rudder that everyone should be using.

It really is all employees using the same criteria from the strategy to evaluate alternatives and make decisions from the wheelhouses they manage. Equipping employees with criteria empowers them to take initiative and be accountable to the greater goals of the company.

So what to do?

Today's environment for companies involved in everything from coal to cupcakes is changing too rapidly to leave things to an annual event. Regardless of your size, geographic location or industry segment, leaving strategy to an event-focused activity does its potential a disservice.

To avoid these "lack of process" pitfalls, you need to have a common, visible and transportable set of steps not only to set strategy but refine it and make mid-course corrections. A sound **Strategy Process** should satisfy the criteria in Table 2.1.

At a very basic level, a sound strategy process should be separated into four visible, meaningful parts or phases. The reason for this is that the thinking is different in each part. The phases should include the components shown in Figure 2.2.

Table 2.1 Criteria to select and benefits of a strategy process

Criteria	Process benefits and attributes
Repeatable	• It is replicable and increases the speed and quality of decision-making. It's not a new flavor every year.
Intuitive	• It must make sense and tells a story. It should be the basis to communicate with a wide range of stakeholders – from the board to the shop floor.
Universal	• It is valid for any size of company or industry. It can be used for your corporate, division or business unit (BU) – it can even be distilled down to a country, sales territory or region.
Selective	• It should automatically collect, arrange and sort relevant from irrelevant data and identify what is missing.
Question driven	• Questions are management tools that channel thinking – key questions should underpin both the major strategy phases and BIG DECISION points in any strategic process.

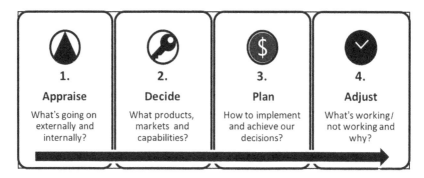

Figure 2.2 Four basic components of a robust strategy process

It should be noted that a solid strategy process, although illustrated in a linear fashion, is **really more iterative and dynamic** than simply one, two three, four . . . done. The process should raise critical questions, uncover gaps, and demand synthesis and soak time as teams work through it.

Because of the velocity of change across industries and the globe – whether it's competition, capital or a short-attention-span workforce that shifts between companies – for the sake of stability and effectiveness, a common process (your process for strategy) should be adopted and made visible.

Having a process versus event approach to strategy ensures that the systems and recipes your company uses to assess, develop, implement and monitor its strategy become part of your organizational way of doing things. It's a bankable driver for scale, sustainability and profitability.

 Now what

If your company has no common, replicable and visible process for strategy, it handcuffs the profit-generating potential. Strategy as a one-time event sets the expectation that it is not important to your company and implies your leadership team can conjure up this competency during predestined times on a corporate calendar. Seasoned executives all have a strategy process in their tool kits to move the company forward – faster, with more alignment and with greater results.

If your company does not have a process, take these actions to remove this Gap:

1　Check to see if you have a common, transportable process for setting and testing strategy; if not . . .
2　Develop or adopt one that integrates these four dimensions:
  •　Appraise
  •　Decide
  •　Plan
  •　Adjust
3　Ensure your process is tied to the fiscal calendar and cadence of your company and is used to assess performance and make mid-course corrections.

3 Outsourcing strategy

Don't bypass sweat equity

 After 5pm

The executives, managers and employees you work with know more about the company's issues than any outsider. Targeted expertise and objective feedback are always welcome, but if you want to set and really implement a strategy to achieve results, you must use those people who understand the nuances and can sweat collectively through the decisions. They will then author and own the outcomes.

Executives are tired of reading decks that contain their own fed-back thinking. CEO takeaway: create a strategy with your own executives and people. Don't outsource it.

Strategy is more important than ever in our rapidly changing, hyper-customized, technology-fueled, got-to-know-now world. Waiting for someone else to give your company the **"silver strategy bullet solution"** is not the answer. By the time you get the answer, something will have changed!

Executives need proximity to issues that impact their strategy so responses can be measured, meaningful and timely. To be close to issues – and solutions – you must be or have been part of the team that sweated through the appraisal and resolution.

You must be the one who put the heavy thinking in, participated in the heated debates and signed off on or agreed to the decisions around products, markets and capabilities that make up your strategy. This process of strategic thinking must not be outsourced.

Consultants who prescribe strategic answers to your company's problems don't work, for these four reasons.

1 More than 80 percent of Gaps holding back your business are known

Yes, it's true.

The core issues that stop a company from succeeding (i.e., profitable and sustained growth) are already known by the majority of people in your company. If the issues are known, you don't need a prescriptive consultant repackaging the issues – you need your best people working collaboratively to understand, prioritize and solve them.

Most insider secrets or success factors that are contained in consulting reports on your industry were generated from conversations with key people from your company to begin with.

So why pay for what is already yours?

Recommendations from strategy consultants seem nice and neat, but rarely get implemented because they are not authored or owned by the people in your company.

Caveat

Content strategy consultants (CSCs) and Subject Matter Experts (SMEs) are truly valuable when you and your executive team have specific identified data gaps – and can ask them very specific questions to get the information you need as an input to the decisions that must be made by your team.

2 The right answer may not be right for your company

No one can replace your thinking and executive sweat when creating a strategy. It's like saying I will skip the maternity phase but just enjoy the baby at the end. For those of you with kids, you know what I mean.

In setting strategy – which is a blend of discipline and creativity – it's unwise to have someone take an off-the-shelf solution and tell you to copy it or recreate it for your business. On paper it looks good, but in reality we know that what's not written is the underlying culture, capabilities and company DNA that ends up being the differentiator for success, which may not be part of who your company is.

So the strategy prescribed looks good, but in your gut you know it's not the fit. The right answer is not the right answer for your company – and your people know it.

Caveat

There are strategic tools on how to compete that are helpful to stimulate strategic thinking . . . but they are principles and do not prescribe your exact future. Only you can do this effectively for your company.

3 Strategic prescription creates resentment with key players in your firm

- **"I could have told them that"**
- **"Let's see them implement this"**
- **"That solution won't work with our culture"**

These words (or their equivalent) I always hear, without fail, when executives have been working with a prescriptive strategy consultant.

Now these might not be the most mature responses, but executives and managers, who have invested years in the business and know the issues, want to be part of the solution. And while everyone puts on a brave face when the strategy is unveiled to the management team after six months of work and $1 million in fees, the reality is a slow, smoldering burn of resentment awash in many parts of the organization.

The downside to prescriptive strategy consulting is CEOs end up spending time gaming the strategy with top executives whom they know are not so "hot" on the solution. This approach takes more energy than just engaging those who are closest to the issues and need to own the changes for the company to really implement the strategy anyway.

Caveat

In every strategy that works, some people need to be changed out because new skills and capabilities are needed. However, it's critical to understand that you can avoid much of the anxiety around changes that come from setting and implementing a new strategy if you involve those who need to live it on a daily basis.

4   Left holding the implementation bag

As a proud owner of a new prescribed strategy, you flip through the 212-page PowerPoint deck and, when you get to the last page, it says, "All this can be yours for 1 million USD." This ploy really irritates executives I have worked with. It reminds them of the "bait and switch" method. But many leaders go ahead and pay it to no avail because they are either too far into the project or don't have the bite to say no.

If you outsource your strategic thinking, the changes required are not authored by the very people who need to lead this change. Bottom line: you should involve ***your people*** in strategy development and implementation to get results.

Caveat

There are great coaches, catalysts and project-management methodologies that consultants can bring in and you should consider when implementing your strategy. But the distinction is that they are helping package and process the activities that have been created by you . . . you still own the thinking. See Table 3.1 for criteria for evaluating consultants.

Table 3.1 Criteria to evaluate prescriptive or process consultants

Checklist to evaluate consultants – you can use all or some of these to evaluate potential consultants   *This is a decision – weigh the criteria (10 = most important to 1 = least important) and then evaluate your consultant alternatives*

Weight 10–1	*Consultant criteria to evaluate*
	Do they engage stakeholders? Evaluate the degree to which their strategy process challenges and engages all critical stakeholders for inputs – from the board of directors to employee – and helps the CEO to manage up and down during the engagement.
	Do they set a baseline? Evaluate if their process establishes a commonly agreed baseline of where you currently are relative to strategic issues and future needs.
	Do they describe their value? Evaluate the degree their proposal outlines the understanding and impact of the work to be performed relative to the fees or retainer.
	What is the rigor of their strategy process? Evaluate the degree their strategy process and tools is battle tested and proven – are these abstract concepts or common sense tools?

(Continued)

Table 3.1 (Continued)

Checklist to evaluate consultants – you can use all or some of these to evaluate potential consultants
This is a decision – weigh the criteria (10 = most important to 1 = least important) and then evaluate your consultant alternatives

---

Weight 10–1	*Consultant criteria to evaluate*

Do they have the expertise you are looking for?
Evaluate the degree of expertise and experience of the consultants who will be working on the type of need you have and ensure they don't downsource to junior consultants.

Do they have CEO references?
Evaluate and ask for CEO references about their process and resources – a CEO-to-CEO talk goes a long way to sharing value delivered.

Do they have quantified EBITDA results with clients?
Evaluate and ask if they have delivered EBITDA outcomes to clients from their strategic process and work – it's about profit, not activities completed.

How practical and transferrable is their process?
Evaluate the degree their tools can be transferred and embedded in the organization to drive decision-making by your executives and employees.

Do they integrate financial analysis?
Evaluate the degree to which their strategy process uses financial analysis (your teams or theirs) to make product, market and capability decisions that drive, support or refute potential competitive advantages.

How do they describe sustainability of the process?
Evaluate their strategy process relative to how systematic and repeatable it is so you can use it after the consultants are gone.

How does their process build accountability?
Evaluate how well their process must deliver clear goals, metrics and targets the executive team and organization can be held accountable for.

How does their process integrate external environment and competition factors?
Evaluate how well their process ensures decision factors in current and future competition and regulatory, technical and societal dimensions.

If you are thinking of using a prescriptive consultant versus one who provides a proven process, facilitates the team and then embeds the process as something to use during the year, consider using Table 3.1 to evaluate potential consultants.

Now what

Bypassing sweat equity is strongly discouraged. If you want a strategy that leverages the best experience in the industry, those resources most likely reside in your company.

Actions:

1   If you need to use a PRESCRIPTIVE strategy consultant or subject matter expert (SME), use your strategy process to clearly define the questions you need answered by them.
2   If you still don't want to develop the strategy yourself, use the check-list process in Table 3.1 to evaluate your options and value for dollars invested.

Caveat

You still need people in the organization to buy in and own the strategy – if they don't create the strategy but consultants do, prepare yourself for the effort required to get your top executives back on board.

4 Forgetting about profit

Why is there no vice president of profitability?

 After 5pm

Profit is good. It's the absolute hard dollar output. Profitability is better – it's the return on resources that creates those hard dollars. Profitability keeps businesses sustainable and enables companies to reinvest or distribute wealth to owners. Too many times, data used to drive decisions is only known at the Gross Margin level, which is not granular enough to make Product by Market decisions. This Gross Margin approach must be avoided, as it skews where and how money is actually being made.

Further complicating this is a common belief that all your people know the workings of a P&L.

Profit is an outcome of Revenue minus Cost; these dimensions need to be taught or reskilled in organizations. Silo effect, legacy in operational roles and general lack of P&L experience have built a profit blindside into the decision-making and actions of many executives and employees.

Few CEOs care to admit it, but the simple *Revenue-Cost=Profit* equation is not as clearly understood by P&L owners as it should be. After all you don't directly manage Profit, which is why there is no vice president of profitability. This Gap needs to be fixed in many organizations.

We know that profit (hard dollars, not percentages) makes the world go and it provides the medium to reinvest for future growth.

So why don't companies have a vice president of profitability?

Organizations don't have VPs of profitability because we actually don't manage profit directly. It's the output of the activities that produce Revenue (Sales) less the activities that it costs to make and support the delivery and service of this product to the customer.

This answer may be obvious to you and those in your company, but I see a profound and practical opportunity for executives and managers who have not yet instilled to key P&L owners that profit (P) is an output of Revenue (R) less Costs (C). R–C=P.

Yes, they are charged and accountable for delivering on the Profit (P), but they often overlook the full range of Revenue and Cost levers they have at their disposal.

As a simple exercise, provide your team with the graphic in Figure 4.1 and ask them to define as many alternatives or actions they have within their arsenal for each of the REVENUE and COST categories they can possibly take to impact Profit.

What we typically see is a few ideas populated in Revenue (e.g., Pricing strategies or Marketing ploys) to raise Volume and, in the C area, things related to Labor or Materials – far from the broader range of alternatives that are available and should be considered.

The second pattern of output that emerges is as follows: if the P&L leader has a Sales, Marketing or DEMAND generation background, they normally default to all things R to fix the bottom-line Profit. Similarly, as expected, someone who has mostly operational experience skews their responses to the C side.

The point is that a P&L owner should have the knowledge and resources of the full arsenal of Profit-improving tools at their disposal to at least consider.

Tim Cook, the CEO of Apple, recently underscored this point, as shown in Figure 4.2.

If a company of Apple's size and profitability can emphasize this – there's little stopping you from at least considering it for your company as well.

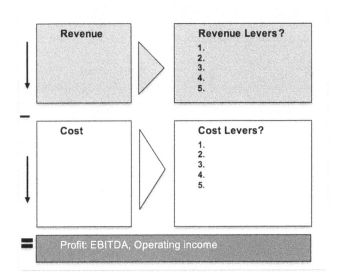

Figure 4.1 Exercise #1: testing profit proficiency with the RCP Framework

> **And so, we're actually not focused on numbers, we're focused on the things that produce the numbers, right?**
>
> **Tim Cook - Apple CEO**

Figure 4.2 Quote by Tim Cook

Source: www.ceo.com/flink/?lnk=http%3A%2F%2Ffortune.com%2F2015%2F02%2F11%2Fapple-ceo-tim-cooks-big-week%2F&id=323745

Five powerful reasons why you should educate or remind your company on where profit comes from

1 Many don't know or have forgotten the simplicity of R–C=P

In the weekly, monthly, quarterly and yearly repetition of reporting, executives and employees can get numb to the intent of the numbers. Many are so focused on getting the report to the people above them that they forget the business is still about getting the right product to the right customer and ensuring the R–C=P equation ends up being positive.

Reminding them of this simple equation or relationship helps declutter thinking and empowers them to take action on things that really matter.

After all, reporting is not a profession – it is a method to exchange relevant data so the managers and management can take action, not admire or fret about the slope or color of graphs.

2 You create stronger teams: everyone serves R, C or both

So much has been written on cross-functional silos and the need to break them down, but by educating your company on how the numbers work, you will naturally break down silos.

This is critical for speed in decision-making, responsiveness to customer problems and simplifying communication in the organization. You will begin to eliminate the Marketing versus Sales, Sales versus Operations and Managers versus Employee disconnects.

It addition, underscoring R–C=P sends a strong message about what **WE** as a company are doing and how **WE** as a company are keeping score on Profit. We are all part of the one success equation.

3 You get better specificity to find why profit is down or up

Two things I always hear in companies when working with executives and managers are:

- "We missed our numbers"
- "We beat the numbers"

and I always ask:

Do you know why? The actual root cause of the result?

The group that has missed the numbers is busy ruffling through reports and papers and the group that made the numbers is sitting back and sipping coffee. In both cases, the groups should know the cause – they should be able to point to the activities that created the surplus or shortfall. And most times they don't.

Too many companies let general answers suffice, such as:

- "We lost key customers" (R is affected)
- "Our suppliers unexpectedly raised prices" (C is affected)

If you teach your executives and employees about the things that make up Revenue (e.g., Volume, Price, Value Proposition, Mix, Competitive Offerings) and Costs (e.g., direct Material and Labor, Indirect Costs, Overhead), they are more apt to get to cause, get you as the leader the right information to make a more informed decision and, importantly, understand that they have more impact on profit than they ever imagined.

4   *Most come up through functional ranks and have not managed a P&L*

We see this situation all the time and it's worth stating again. Many if not most great performers in companies who rise to lead business units, regions or even the company have earned their stripes from a functional or operational start.

Most have not managed a P&L through their entire careers. So it's only natural for certain functions to be focused on Revenue (e.g., new sales, new products, new customer, add-on sales) or, from an operations side, Cost (e.g., inventory or labor above budget, throughput versus goal, scrap rates).

5   *You get an opportunity to share where operational indicators originate*

Many managers and executives give no second thought to where or what spawned operational indicators they routinely report on. Many of these indicators are driven from the very nature of the Income Statement that captures the P&L of the business. But this link of logic tends to be overlooked or disconnected from the business. Financials are for finance people and let me just run my functional area!

Many employees believe such things as Scrap Rate Reporting, Labor Variances and Volume indicators are just plucked from the sky of options – rather than understanding the executive team has deliberately selected these indicators to monitor and manage because they are an important part of the system of activities that makes the company profit.

Evaluating the origins of your operational indicators, driven from the levers that impact the R and C, is a very powerful tool and exercise to confirm they are meaningful and still the best gauge of performance.

So what to do?

RCP is a strategic and operational tool to highlight, track, and systematically connect performance indicators to profit. This tool ensures implications are understood and the full range of levers within a P&L owner's decision-making arsenal are considered to optimize Profitability.

If some of the five reasons described earlier resonate with Gaps you see in your organization, a simple solution to fill this R-C=P competency or confusion is to build upon the earlier exercise and provide a broader range of alternatives that P&L owners should consider, as outlined in a fully depicted RCP Framework below (see Figure 4.3).

This framework, along with the overlay of your company's existing operational indicators, is a powerful one-pager of learning that ensures full exposure to what's available to impact the bottom line and to plug P&L gaps in organization.

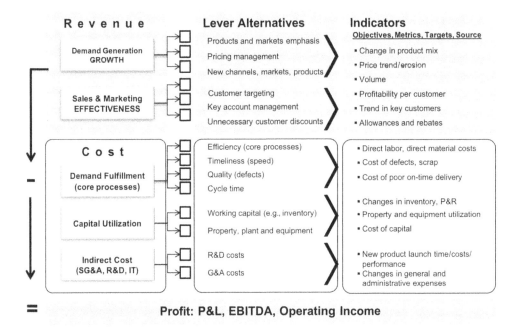

 **Profit: P&L, EBITDA, Operating Income**

Figure 4.3 Exercise #2: share levers and test indicator origins with the RCP framework

---

◇ Now what

RCP is a strategic and operational tool to highlight, track and systematically connect performance levers to profit. This decision-making tool can help to fill in competency Gaps and ensure the full range of areas P&L owners manage are being considered to maximize Profitability. If you have Gaps, take these four group or individual actions:

1   Construct RCP Framework
2   Conduct Exercise 1
3   Conduct Exercise 2
4   Compare to what you have now and make the changes.

Put the learning and outcomes of those RCP applications back into your business to raise P&L competencies and maximize options to generate profit.

5 Mixed up on metrics

When was the answer ever
"have more metrics"?

 After 5pm

Companies are more performance focused and awash in data sources than any time in the history of business. The BIG DATA push seems to amplify this. This data overload and urgency to use more data is compounded by weak fundamentals in organizations for how to build sound indicators that consider the intent, metric, target and data source.

The result: too many metrics get put into too many reports that don't get effectively used to manage POSITIVE and NEGATIVE variations in performance.

CEOs must downsize their metrics to the critical few. Companies should have no more than six to eight strategic indicators.

Ask this question to your top leadership team:

How many monthly reports are generated and never used?
The answer usually comes back – **TOO MANY!**

Complexity and unwarranted complications are killing strategy in organizations. Not because of the size or breadth of the company, but the felt need that strategy should be complex and should involve multi-page, multi-concept and multi-meeting reports or presentations. And overuse or misuse of metrics is a leading cause of this complexity.

Metrics are defined as: **standards for measuring or evaluating something**.

The issue we see in companies is that the "evaluating something" in the definition above has not been thought through. Once metrics are cloaked in importance, the reports begin to pile on, dashboards spring up and soon an inordinate amount of time and resources are consumed to create reports that are never used.

Metrics should be part of the management process to assess performance and use data to determine actions that will enable them to prioritize issues, solve problems and make decisions that affect performance.

This all sounds well and good on paper, but we see much confusion and redundancy when companies share their thinking and approach to metrics.

Here are three major Gaps and three simple solutions to clear the metric confusion in your organization

1   No clear definition or format for metrics

Simply talking "metrics" seems to conjure up competence. But in reality metrics (or the gauge, calibration, parameter) are only one small part in defining performance indicators. The takeaway is that metrics are a good placeholder word, but you have to define what they are in your company.

2   Too many metrics

I see pages and pages of reports in companies that look good and employ the right software or dashboard, but when asked how they are being used, there is no clear consensus.

This is draining, as collecting data on metrics takes resources – time, money and people– and if they are not being used to drive problem-solving and decision-making, it's a real waste of valuable assets.

3   Not separating strategic and operational performance metrics

Every time I see Key Performance Indicators (KPIs) I cringe because, in many cases, this is a long list that contains both Strategic and Operational metrics all mixed together.

Although they may include valuable pieces of information on things being measured, there is no systematic way the company fits them together. Many times, these mixed KPIs can even cannibalize one another.

For example, a functional indicator drives new product launches at the expense of a profitability indicator. Alternatively the number of sales calls per day are at odds with the number of key customer sales calls that should be happening. KPIs need to be distinguished between the WHAT (strategy) and HOW (operations) of a business.

Importantly, these counter-facing metric gaps are critical to fix, because it's likely your compensation programs align themselves with some sort of KPIs and if those don't make strategic sense – supported by aligned operational capabilities that are being measured – you create confusion in your organization about performance priorities.

So what to do

Here are three powerful, yet simple, steps to clarify metrics – or, better stated, performance indicators

1   Do away with the lexicon of KPIs

KPIs are ambiguous.

What is KEY anyway?

If you delve into this, it will surely be some mix of strategy and operational factors. Instead, separate KEY into STRATEGIC (WHAT the business measures) and OPERA-TIONAL (HOW it is accomplishing this).

Table 5.1 Four dimensions of a practical performance indicator

A well-defined and pragmatic indicator always meets these four dimensions that need to be agreed upon by those using them to measure performance

1 Objectives	2 Metric	3 Target, Actual and Gap	4 Data Source
• **What performance is important to get feedback on?** • **What is the intent?**	• What is the metric, gauge or form of calibration that will provide the best information?	• What is the numerical target, range or standard we are trying to achieve? • What is our actual to date?	• What is the agreed-upon data source and frequency of reporting that we need?
Example: Sales Growth	• % Change Year over Year (YOY)	• 20 Target • 10 Actual • (gap is 10)	• Sales Report A provided first of each month

2   Ensure you can check off these four points for any indicator

Try the format in Table 5.1 and you will most likely see there may not even be clear definitions or agreement on which of these four points is OK – but you need to clarify them because it is this lack of clarity that is causing the disconnects (and the overzealous reports being generated).

3   Divorce strategic from operational indicators

Strategic indicators should be key data points that give your executive team and organization feedback that their strategy is working as envisioned.

Most C-Suite and seasoned executives intuitively know that no strategy ever developed is 100 per cent correct. There is no guarantee or executive crystal ball that states the hard decisions they made around Products, Market and Capabilities will unfold as expected every time.

This accepted risk is what CEOs are rightfully paid for and underscores why you need to have Strategic Performance Indicators (SPIs) or specific feedback points that can indicate what is working and not working.

Every company should really have **no more than six to eight SPIs** that they monitor quarterly or monthly. SPIs should be created from the fundamental decision points behind the purpose and path for your company, including Financial, Products (services), Markets (geographies, channels, Customers) and Capabilities (processes and competencies) you made when setting your strategy.

You should consider no more than two indicators for each of the four categories (note: examples are provided in each bullet point):

Lagging indicators:

1   Financial (LAGGING)
- Revenue
- Net Income

2   Customer/Product (LAGGING)
- Key Product Segments
- Key Market Segments Sales/Penetration/Profit Volume

Leading indicators:

3   Process (LEADING) – key competencies that create advantage
- Number of new product launches
- Number of days for delivery

4   People (LEADING)
- Individual Performance Objectives
- Alignment of Behaviors to Values/Basic Beliefs

This set of metrics has a strong link of **Cause and Effect** that reinforces that PEOPLE, through processes, create PRODUCTS for CUSTOMERS that pay you REVENUE so you take home PROFIT. That's really why many seasoned CEOs put PEOPLE as their number one priority! **People constitute the foundation for performance.**

Data is critical for decision-making and metrics form a key point of feedback that must be clarified and simplified to make organizations stronger.

But the "buzz" around metrics needs to be sorted or you may be relying on collecting and using data to guide corrections in your business that have no basis on what is actually driving performance and profit.

 Now what

Mixed up on metrics needs to be corrected. You know your company is mixed up or is at least deficient in choosing and using the correct performance indicators to provide valuable feedback if you ask for a show of hands in response to the question "Do we have too many reports?" and the answer comes back "Yes." Actions you can take to remove this Gap:

1   **Separate SPIs from operational performance indicators (OPIs)**
2   **Use objective, metric, target and data source format**
3   **Instill the point that indicators are about using relevant data to find root cause of surpluses and shortfalls in Revenue, Cost and Profitability – and take the appropriate actions or make the needed decisions.**

6 Vague Latitude

Assumed buy-in from boards
to employees

 After 5pm

Setting strategy is a difficult endeavor – not gathering parameters from the parent, board or owners before embarking on its development is a disaster. In many cases, CEOs surmise the parameters or criteria for any option the board might consider – only to find out during the board meeting that their strategic growth option does not fit what the board had in mind.

CEOs need to ensure they have a visible one-pager of dimensions that define what's in or out BEFORE setting strategy. In many cases, the board is thankful this dialogue is established and clear lines of Strategic Latitude are established.

The downfall of not capturing these expectations is a world of effort to develop strategic alternatives that can be quickly voided when a board member growls in a meeting that inorganic growth was never to be included as a part of the strategy unless it is self-funded in the first place!

Does your company have Strategic Latitude guidelines?

Boards play a critical role in lending their earned experience and advising CEOs on how best to navigate strategic opportunities and pitfalls. Boards should expect a clear strategy from the CEO that explicitly shows the rationale of product, market and capability choices being made to propel the company to its EBITDA targets. Conversely, CEOs should receive a clear set of parameters or boundaries to use in setting the strategy.

In practice the board/CEO exchange on Strategic Latitude is often assumed and murky. Consequently board members and CEOs end quarterly meetings with more questions than answers. It sometimes takes the team dinner after the meeting to figure out what really is causing consternation from the board.

To side step this expectation gap (and this gap, if left unchecked, can have an enormous detrimental impact on EBITDA performance, the speed and quality of decision-making, and the tenure of the CEO), I suggest a one-page document called **Strategic Latitude** that every CEO and board needs to co-create and audit.

1   *Strategic Latitude: what is it?*

Strategic Latitude is a one-page document that asks and answers:

- **What parameters, boundaries and expectations must be adhered to both in setting the strategy and achieving results?**

The format should include objectives (with relative weights), metrics, targets and data sources for each of the parameters being set forth by the board.

   In practice this is an iterative exchange. It is best for the board to provide this assignment to the CEO and executive team at the start of a strategic setting process because its helps to narrow or widen the strategic alternatives being considered. Most importantly, it points out Gaps and areas of alignment that can be shored up to avoid future disconnects.

2   *Questions and categories to create your Strategic Latitude document*

A simple way to facilitate the creation of this document is to ask the four questions shown in Figure 6.1:

- **When we devise our strategy, what are the stakeholder...**

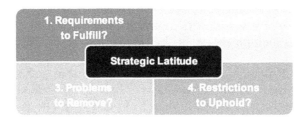

Figure 6.1 Strategic Latitude questions

The output of the questions in Figure 6.1 typically reveals these types of objectives that should be weighted on *a relative scale to each of the other objectives* (1=low to 10=high):

- Strategic Time Frame
- Scale on Exit
- Cash Flow
- EBITDA per year
- Capital Available for Projects
- Growth by Product Line or Market (or both)
- Inorganic Spend for Acquisitions
- Product/Market Concentration and Change
- Core Competencies to Maintain
- New Competencies built to drive Margin or scale Advantage
- Risk Tolerance (Probability and impact profile of decision-making that is acceptable)
- Generation considerations (if family owned)

Weight	Objective	Metric	Target
10	Overall business scale on exit	EBITDA on exit	>X million
10	Cash flow positive	Free cash flow $	>X million
8	Drive growth in profitable product lines	Product A Product B Product C Product D	>X% >X% >X% >X%
8	Drive high-performance culture	# of high-performing individuals	≥ X% of the workforce
6	Capital available for projects	ROI	X years or less
3	Maximum capital available	Annual investment limit per fiscal year of hold	2014 ≤ $X million 2015 ≤ $X million 2016 ≤ $X million
8	Future growth	# of new products	> 5 new products per year
5	Maintain focus on core skills	Manufacturing technologies	X
5	Increase share of proprietary products	% revenues in proprietary products	
7	Reduction in geographical market concentration	% share in EMEA and International	EMEA: >X International: >10

Figure 6.2 Sample Strategic Latitude with Objectives, Metrics and Targets

Figure 6.2 offers a sample format that can be used to create a Strategic Latitude one-pager for your company and board to collaboratively create and importantly use as guardrails. Strategic Latitude offers three powerful benefits:

- It helps the board provide *specific guidance on performance* during the year to the CEO and executive team.
- It sets *clear accountability for* performance and in many cases compensation and/or long-term incentive plans (LTIPs).
- It is an input to ensure Strategic and Operational Indicators developed during the strategy sessions back-cast to achieving stated aims (i.e., you measure the right things for the right outcomes).

As you set expectations for your strategy, create a Strategic Latitude document to ensure all stakeholders are aligned.

 Now what

Strategic Latitude is simply a set of objectives with defined metrics, targets (or ranges) and data sources for what dimensions a company can use to develop a strategy. Actions to consider:

1 **Take the initiative to engage stakeholders and create a Strategic Latitude one-pager with input from your leadership team**
2 **Use the OBJECTIVE, METRIC, TARGET, SOURCE FORMAT**
3 **Bring it to the board as first-pass thinking for them to audit and edit**
4 **Get confirmation before starting on strategy development**
5 **Use this latitude list as an additional reference to build and share the strategy story for your stakeholders.**

Part II

BUILD

A simple strategy system to make big decisions better

7 Introduction to TDG's strategy system

What to create, why and how

 After 5pm

Profitability and Performance are monitored and fixed with the following tools:

1 Tool 1: Assumptions and Implications
2 Tool 2: Product Market Capability (PMC) Engine
3 Tool 3: Goals and Gaps

   These three tools form the basis of a simple, proven and put-to-use system employed by our clients. This system enables CEOs to have three one-page tools to set strategy, make better decisions, adjust for course corrections and apportion scarce resources to areas that have the greatest impact on their companies.

Six **Gaps** in strategy were outlined at the start of the book.

1 The absence of shared language: why no one is on the same page
2 Mistaken identity: strategy is a decision-making process, not an event
3 Outsourcing strategy: don't bypass sweat equity
4 Forgetting about profit: why is there no vice president of profitability?
5 Mixed up on metrics: when was the answer ever "have more metrics"?
6 Vague Latitude: assumed buy-in from boards to employees

All of these are real and all are fixable, but nonetheless blockers to better strategy and predictable profitability, which is the aim of this book.

The solution is laid out so you as executive practitioners and P&L owners can create and quickly put to use this simple system to make big decisions better and engrain a consistent way of setting and delivering results for your business (see Figure 7.1).

These strategy system tools are so intuitive and powerful because they are based on the fundamental, simple and hard-wired thinking patterns in all of us – looking at cause, making choices and thinking ahead about risks (see Figure 7.2).

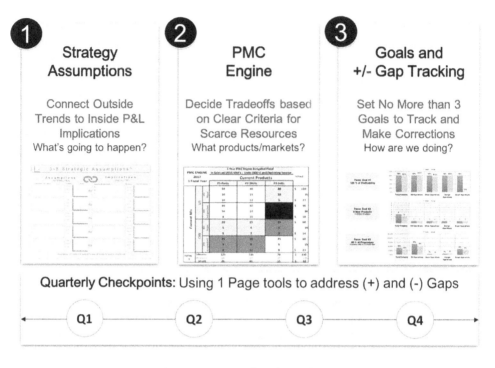

Figure 7.1 TDG Strategy System: three one-pager tools underpin the CEO control center to lead, manage and monitor performance

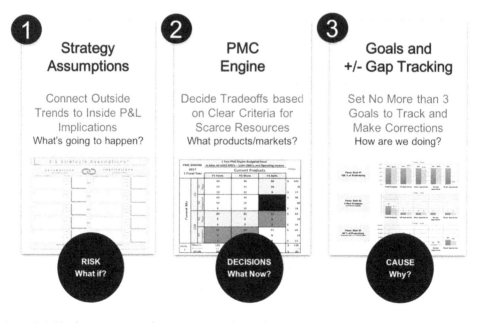

Figure 7.2 Thinking patterns and intuitive intent that underpin the TDG Strategy System tools

Table 7.1 Value and context of TDG Strategy System tools

Tool	Purpose	Promotes	Prevents
1 Strategic Assumptions	• Connect outside to inside and understand the probability and impact	• Identifying and quantifying the critical few external forces that matter for your company's profitability	• Being in the weeds or too internally focused
2 PMC Engine	• Criteria-driven priorities to direct product-market and capability decisions	• Deciding where to place current and future bets using clear criteria against scarce resources to maximize profitability	• Ad hoc, differing or unfocused decision-making by the C-Suite and managers
3 Goals and Gaps	• Fixate on the few goals and find cause for variations	• Align all employees' efforts to what matters; understand why positive or negative gaps are occurring	• Diffused focus and energy on the wrong things, guessing at cause

The value and context for use of each tool are outlined in Table 7.1.

The simplicity of this system is its power because it gets to the actionable heart of strategy, keeps it uncomplicated and, no matter the size of the organization, you will keep people focused on the critical few things that matter. In short: your executive team can actually use it and will want to.

While this may be termed an oversimplification to all the different tools and buzz words in strategy, I would and do err on the side of **simple, understandable and owned** – which is what these tools provide your organization.

The essence and output of this system is three one-pagers:

1   **Strategic Assumption and Implications**: the future
    The three to five EXTERNAL forces that your team believes will unfold during its strategic time frame and provide the pivot point to make INTERNAL choices on what to do and not do relative to your product, market, and capability alternatives.
2   **PMC Engine**: the decision hub
    A single-page economic decision-making tool that visibly shows your Product, Market and Capability choices (your strategy) and the rationale behind their relative priority.
    The PMC Engine illustrates where you choose to play and profit based on external and internal reality along with your path for growth. It becomes real because it contains the Revenue, Profit and Volume for each Product/Market cell in a SHOULD/ACTUAL reporting format as you use it in your strategy.
3   **Goals and Gaps**: reality check to monitor and make changes
    Three goals with clear metrics, targets and data source that underpin the strategic aim of your company for one calendar year; on and to which everyone in the company is concentrated and connected, above all else.
    Their achievement assures success for the organization for that year. They reinforce the competency and requirement of truly finding cause for over- or underperformance.

Value and power of TDG's Strategy System

With these three one-pagers (see Figure 7.1), you can manage, monitor and make critical decisions and, importantly, always ask the vital questions to understand why your business is delivering the result it is. These tools connect the external environment to your internal choices and specifically the few goals that define success.

The reality of any company is that financial performance is the sum total of daily decisions made by each person. The quality and consistency of those decisions represent 100 per cent of its EBITDA potential.

The seemingly elusive ability to make aligned and consistent individual decisions is more essential than ever in the wake of industry dynamics, global change and overwhelming amounts of data.

These three tools will equip your C-Suite and executive team with a common and quantified decision-making hub to enhance strategic thinking and decision-making competencies to gain your right share of profit.

 Now what

Scholars and theorists of strategy can argue all day on the complexity and nuances of strategy. But for C-Suite, executive practitioners and P&L owners, we don't have that luxury.

We need a few good tools to help us set the purpose and path of our company and test if the decisions we made are sound and working to drive predictable Profitability.

Don't overthink strategy or wait to take these steps to a better business:

1   Absorb why these three pillars are the essence of any strategy
2   Read the next three chapters and create the system for your firm
3   Engage your leadership team to help you construct them.

---

8 Strategic Assumptions and Implications

Connect outside to inside

 After 5pm

Strategic Assumptions force an "outside to in" view of your business. This ability to systematically look outside your business and identify the Opportunities and Threats is critical. The strange thing about strategy is decisions that are or may be paramount to your business can go unnoticed unless you are actively searching for them. Assumptions do just that.

Every strategy is based on some set of assumptions or vision of how the future will unfold. These insights, instincts or beliefs about a certain opportunity, niche play or unmet customer gap spawn from distilling the outside noise to the unique combinations of company strengths and abilities that leaders believe they can configure to exploit or mitigate them.

The trouble is, many companies and leadership teams operate with implicit or unchallenged assumptions that end up driving decisions for good or bad. Further, they over-glorify how strong and unique their strengths really are. Both are recipes for disaster.

CEOs need to identify the five to eight forces and factors they believe will unfold, quantify them and draw out the parallel internal choices – product, market and capabilities – that will mitigate and/or exploit those forces.

Every strategy sits on a bed of Strategic Assumptions.

How known, visible, agreed-upon or used are your assumptions?

It is impossible for any CEO or executive team to make decisions that are not based on some point of view, gut feeling or data of how they believe the "world will unfold" in relation to their industry.

Think of the different versions of reality the executives of Boeing's Dreamliner 787 versus Airbus A380 had. What about Uber's assumptions compared to those of car rental companies and taxis?

Because they have different "versions of how the world will unfold," they have naturally made contrasting investments in the Product, Market and Capabilities choices based on their version of the future for the SUPPLY and DEMAND of their industries.

Who's right – as measured by sustainable profitability – only time will tell; but you can see clear choices based on Strategic Assumptions very evident here.

The assumption Gap CEOs need to close

The breach we see with executive thinking is not in the "strategic assumption itself" but the inability to leverage their vast expertise, experience and insight that sits within but remains widely dispersed across their company. In short, company leaders 99 times out of 100 know much more about their industry than outsiders – their knowledge just needs to be channeled to practical implications.

The result is that strategic plan creators have no way to test the soundness of their thinking during execution; they often defend erroneous assumptions because there was never any visibility or executive alignment to start with. This defense of unsubstantiated thinking sucks up a lot of executive time in meetings that can be avoided or put to better use.

Rather than **Wait and React**, why not proactively make assumptions visible and test their soundness along the way, thereby giving your company a better approach to displaying the rationale of options and monitoring them to make mid-course corrections? Misuse or non-use of Strategic Assumptions is a recipe for disaster in setting effective corporate strategies.

If this sounds like your organization, use this simple but potent five-step checklist to assess how well your company is applying Strategic Assumptions to guide its decision-making.

1   Understand what Strategic Assumptions are/are not

Assumptions are short statements that display what your executive team believes will unfold in the external environment during your strategic time frame. They are the critical few factors that define success for those who choose to play in this industry. At the most basic business level, they are levers that drive supply and demand. Assumptions are **EXTERNAL** factors, forces or circumstances that affect all firms in the industry.

Figure 8.1 provides an example.

It is very beneficial for your team to draw a small graph to visually "see the prediction" and rate of expected change. This alone spurs constructive strategic debate among senior executives and, importantly, surfaces gaps in thinking. It forces these questions: "WHY do you think that? What is the rationale or insight behind this?"

Strategic Assumptions	
EXTERNAL – Applies to your company and all others in the industry	
Assumption 1:	
• DEMAND: China mobile phone market is between 600-700 million users and <u>will increase</u> at a rate of 10-12% per year till 2019	

Figure 8.1 External part of a Strategic Assumption

If your company uses SWOT Analysis – and many do – this is an excellent tool to put the OPPORTUNITY and THREAT categories to a strategic use or input (rather than lie dormant after a meeting as many do).

2 Quantify and assign a probability to assumptions

Given that assumptions are an expectation of the future that can't be 100 per cent predicted, many organizations say, "Why guess at it?"

We don't recommend you guess, but rather make visible the thinking and quantify your assumptions within some peer-agreed range. You are looking for Order of Magnitude here – not academic precision. Later, deeper analysis or supporting data needs may be needed to support or invalidate your assumption(s). Once you have set Order of Magnitude, assign each assumption:

- **High: H=>75 per cent probability it will happen**
- **Medium: M=50–75 per cent probability it will happen**
- **Low: L=<50 per cent probability it will happen**

as the calibration or use some agreed-upon rating. Figure 8.2 provides an example.

From our experience, executives are more right than wrong in the assumptions of how the industry structure and therefore profitability will unfold in the future. (Over the last 17 years, I would say that 80 per cent of Strategic Assumptions that client teams expressed upon review unfolded as expected.)

3 Link Strategic Assumptions to Implications and quantify each potential implication impact to Sales, Profit and/or ROIC

For each externally based assumption, there are key internal questions, all with the same intent:

A   If this assumption unfolds, SO WHAT? There is usually a wide range of options to consider to address the assumption.
B   Which internal alternatives exist to exploit or mitigate this trend?
C   Which inorganic actions could we consider?
D   What does this assumption mean to our current/future Product-Market mix and required capabilities to protect our advantage?

Strategic Assumptions	
EXTERNAL – Applies to your company and all others in the industry	
Assumption 1:	Probability
DEMAND: China mobile phone market is between 600–700 million users and will increase at a rate of 10–12% per year till 2019	High >75%

Figure 8.2 External part of a Strategic Assumption with Probability

Keep in mind that *Implications are internal options and only apply to your company* (in comparison to Assumptions, which are external)

Because Strategic Assumptions directly impact your Product, Market (read: customer) and Capabilities (read: expertise and processes to invest in), Implications force your team to draw links from the Assumptions to scenarios that may unfold (or are unfolding).

The links from outside to inside enable you to make the rationale visible and develop options for your business. ***Each of these options*** (see Figure 8.3) or business cases should be quantified in terms of at least one or all of the following impacts from an incremental standpoint:

*   Sales and/or Volume
*   Profit (operating income or EBITDA, if possible)
*   Return on Invested Capital (ROIC)

and then calibrated with High, Medium or Low relative to what is relevant to your company (e.g., High Sales Impact may be 100 million for one company whereas High Sales Impact may be 10 million for another).

In practice, my request for the executive to "quantify the impact" of these potential options is met with a grimace. This grimace is based on their thinking that we are too early into the process or they really don't know what the financial case may be.

However, when pressed for a first-hand guesstimate, they usually come up with a meaningful range that will be scrutinized with the appropriate level of financial analysis as the strategy process unfolds.

Strategic Assumptions				
EXTERNAL (FORCES)			**INTERNAL (OPTIONS)**	
ASSUMPTIONS	**Probability** •H= > 75% •M= 50-75% •L= < 50%		**IMPLICATIONS** (OPTIONS TO CONSIDER)	**Potential Incremental Sales Impact** • H=>50MM • M=20-50 MM • L=<20<MM
The China mobile phone market is between 600-700 million users and will increase at a rate of 10-12% per year till 2019	High = >75% 800 700 600 17 18 19		1. **Product** – Develop a new product for the Chinese market	50-60 MMs HIGH
			2. **Market** – Enter China market through acquisition	35-45 MMs MEDIUM
			3. **Capability** – Build an organic sales infrastructure to gain share in China	12-18 MMs LOW

Figure 8.3 A fully developed Strategic Assumption (external) and Implication (internal)

4　*Try to limit your strategy to no more than five to eight Strategic Assumptions*

- More than five to eight Strategic Assumptions usually means you are giving points for quantity rather than quality of thought. Assumptions are really about the SUPPLY and DEMAND of your industry with TECHNOLOGY as the fulcrum for rate of change.
- This means you need to distill the few that really drive and affect the certainty of your industry's supply and demand (i.e., Profitability).

(Note: it's fine to have a lengthy first-pass list of assumptions [10–15], but this should be shortened down to what is meaningful to success in your industry.)

5　*Build your strategy upon the assumptions and test quarterly*

With assumptions now visible and quantified – and with a probability assigned along with the impact to Product, Market and Capabilities choices – you now can leverage these to develop alternative strategies that will allow you to win in the marketplace. You are looking to test the rate and magnitude of change that is occurring. Do you need more or fewer resources to exploit or mitigate trends unfolding?

This is not a robotic step – far from it – but with this data visible, you will highlight areas of opportunity and areas of risk to be mitigated much more readily than not. Because assumptions are just that – forecasts of the future – your company needs to test the validity of your assumptions and associated actions to offer mid-point corrections based on how the world has actually unfolded each quarter and at the very least annually. These five checkpoints will give you and your executives more control over the future than anyone would have predicted. Use the template in Figure 8.4 to capture your thinking.

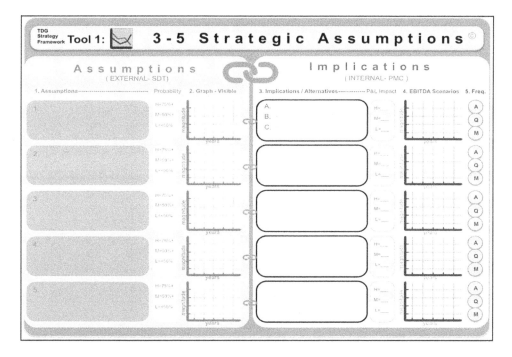

Figure 8.4 Strategic Assumptions and Implications template

⟨?⟩ **Now what**

Strategic Assumptions are your company's brain trust predictions of the future. In most cases your team of executives working together can collectively identify a better picture of the future than an expert.

These insights need to be visible and leveraged to drive better and more profitable decision-making in your company. All strategic decisions pivot from assumptions. You need to extract that value by these actions:

1   Enlist your leadership team or resident experts.
2   Use the template provided in Figure 8.3 and outline five to eight critical EXTERNAL forces that will unfold in your time frame and ask the So What Implication questions for each assumption relative to your product, market and capabilities choices.
3   You need to test assumptions and internal actions at least quarterly as the world unfolds to guide mid-course corrections in your strategy.
4   At the end of the day it's helpful to recognize how the Assumptions-Implications template really illustrates the risk appetite of your company or owners; that is, Probability of the Assumption's X Impact on your business.

9 Product Market Capability (PMC) Engine

Creating the economic control center for setting strategy and making big decisions

 After 5pm

The PMC Engine is the single-page, economic heart, strategic and decision-making tool that powerfully combines and illustrates your product, market and capabilities choices and relative importance. It can be put down on paper with a pencil or embedded in elaborate information systems. The PMC visual should fit your gut or eye for what the business is doing and needs to do.

It is a *prioritizing tool that combines Strategic, Operational and Financial elements on a single page*. It forces financial and data rigor because it holds the Budget and Actual Revenue, Margin and Volume information for each product/market combination that you serve.

It is used to show GROWTH, COMPETITIVE ADVANTAGE and CAPABILITY INVESTMENT decisions and results. It also can show where the initiatives of implementation are focused.

It *serves up the SHOULD versus ACTUAL performance* that puts clear decision-making tools at the fingertips of the C-Suite. And it drives or becomes your company's budget, strategy and long-range planning (LRP) basis.

Every company, business unit, region should have a PMC Engine because it is THE one piece of paper that represents your world and the choices that are your means to achieving your goals.

Do you currently have a one-page strategy tool that:

* **Illustrates** your big Decisions Products, Markets, Capabilities?
* **Shows** relative priority of *all* your products and markets?
* **Highlights** where you make money and don't?
* **Bares** the truth if your competitive advantage is real?
* **Forces** pinpointed dialogue about performance?

The best-performing companies and CEOs do.

In addition, they use the PMC Engine to help answer and communicate to their leadership teams and stakeholders the most vexing questions they all need answers for:

1   **Why?** Why are we winning/losing?
2   **What's first?** What are the relative Product/Market priorities?
3   **What's next?** What are the future options/paths for growth?

If you can't answer these questions, you should consider this an invitation to create a PMC Engine for your company.

The PMC Engine is the central hub and holy grail for strategy because it represents on a single page the three decision pillars of choices: Products, Markets and Capabilities.

It becomes the HEART in the search for Profitability because it allows you to delve into and pinpoint competitive advantage. This advantage is the difference in RELATIVE Price or Cost caused by your chosen activities performed by your company for each Product/Market combination you serve with the assets under your command and control.

The creation of a PMC Engine delivers six powerful benefits (SCORE) in the pursuit of profitable performance. They make your strategic thinking and strategy:

1   **Simple**: single page visual of the High, Medium and Low product market priorities
2   **Clear**: common and standard criteria to evaluate Product, Market and Capabilities alternatives and apportioning scarce resources
3   **Overt**: relevant product and market segments connected to external data
4   **Real**: financial data to chart results, root cause and course corrections
5   **Executable**: initiatives that tie strategy decisions to required actions that build capacities and deliver profit

You may be amazed how powerful making this thinking visible is and helpful it is to fine-tune what each of your leadership team members is focused on. Executives and leaders can quickly assess and improve a company's ability to perform by ensuring they build a PMC Engine.

I can best explain the PMC Engine and show you how it can be used in three separate but integrated parts. Each builds on the others and explaining it this way offers you the greatest flexibility to use the PMC Engine on your most pressing strategic decision-making needs:

PMC Application 1: RELATIVE PRIORITY
Prioritize Product and Markets, and structure essential competitive information needed to make data-driven decisions

PMC Application 2: GROWTH OPTIONS
Identify and evaluate future growth options to sharply determine what's next for the business

PMC Application 3: FUTURE CAPABILITIES
Determine and quantify key Capabilities that will make your strategy real and realistic, and that will provide a base test of the Return on Invested Capital

PMC Application 1: Relative Priority

Prioritize Product and Markets, and structure essential competitive information needed to make data-driven decisions

How to create a PMC Engine

Before we ask you to grab a pencil and consider sketching out a draft of your company's PMC Engine, let's raise the motivation bar on WHY you should consider this.

Picture your leadership team and key decision makers around a table at a normal strategy session and you walk in with a list of questions that, if known and agreed upon, will allow you to move quickly, methodically and deliberately on decision-making and implementation actions for your business. Would they quickly be able to answer these?

Figure 9.1 shows real questions CEOs and P&L owners must be able to answer (and have the same answers for) to effectively have a handle on their business and make the difficult decisions of where to allocate scarce resources and capital.

Each of the questions in Figure 9.1 can be answered using the PMC Engine.

Would My Leadership Team Be Able to Answer These Questions?

1) Which **products and customers** are the most and least profitable?

2) **Why do we sell these products** to the customers we do – and not others?

3) **What criteria** determine which products-markets get scarce resources?

4) Why do we have these **product-market segments** and not different ones?

5) What new product or market will **drive future growth**?

6) What is our inorganic or **M+A roadmap**?

7) What **premium do we capture** for our competitive advantage?

8) Where we **gaining or losing share** – in Sales dollars ($) and volume?

9) Where are we **under attack** from external forces or competition?

10) What is the **rationale for the product-market growth targets set**?

Figure 9.1 Leadership questions answered by the PMC Engine

Steps 1 and 2: create your own company's PMC Engine

To create the PMC Engine, follow these steps:

1   **Define four to six PRODUCT** segments and **four to six MARKET segments** that total 100 per cent of your Revenue, Volume and Profit.

PMC Engine	YOUR Products				
		P1	P2	P3	Pn
YOUR Markets	M1				
	M2				
	M3				
	Mn				

> The PMC Cells Engine Must Total 100% of Your Sales, Volume, and Profit

Figure 9.2 Basic PMC Engine (with no financial data or emphasis)

TIP: Defining meaningful product and market segments requires some CEO judgment, as you do not want the Products and Markets so granular that the matrix becomes overly complex – there is a balance to strike, so you may need a few iterations on this.

Then create a PMC Engine by putting your PRODUCT segments (P1 through Pn) across the top and MARKET (M1 through Mn) segments along the side, as shown in Figure 9.2.

2   Next, **populate** each P1/M1. . . Pn/Mn cell with Revenue, Volume and Profit (Operating Income or Gross Margin) that can be attributed to each PRODUCT-MARKET combination. In practice *many* companies note:

- Hey we don't have data in this format – but can get it with a little work
- We have never looked at it from a "Product-Markets together" perspective
- We can only get the profit data at a GROSS Margin per cent or $ level in a Product-Market format
- This seems so obvious – connecting products to markets – why did we not do it earlier?

Case in point: typical presentations miss connecting products to customer segments

Many companies discuss or report Product and Market performance as separate, distinct entities (see Figure 9.3). The employees or the board end up with two slides, which are less than helpful in connecting Products and Markets.

Each of the graphs is for the same 2015 Sales, but in different ways. These three separate views of the business are accurate but nowhere as powerful or relevant for decision-making as the PMC Engine, which creates the natural, normal and needed link of Product to Market thinking.

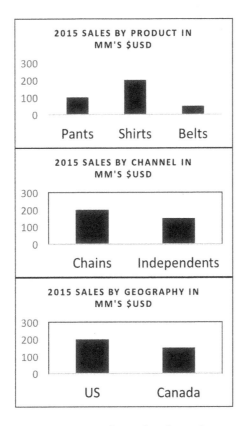

Figure 9.3 The usual way companies present product and market performance: this disconnects the natural product-market relationships

Although this is helpful information and looks great in a PowerPoint slide, does it effectively:

- **Depict** the *relative priority* and strategic importance of each Product-Market combination?
- **Show** where we *strategically* said we were to be emphasizing and investing?
- **Illustrate** the true *relationship* between the product performance, a certain market or customer or channel?
- **Cause** the CEO and leadership to ask *WHY* are we winning or losing in these Product/Market cells?

From my experience the answer with companies we have seen is "NO," but they really would like to answer the above questions.

The graphs look good, but they render the strategy meeting a reporting meeting rather than a resolution work session. We show the data rather than use the data.

But with the PMC Engine, we can change all that quite quickly. The illustration in Figure 9.4 shows a fully constructed PMC Engine population with financial data.

PMC ENGINE 2017 1 Fiscal Year			1 Year PMC Engine Budgeted Fiscal in Sales of $US MMs - Units (000's) and Operating Income $ **Current Products**			Market Totals
			P1-Pants	P2-Shirts	P3-Belts	
Current Markets	US	M1 Major Chains	50	40	30	$ 120
			10	15	10	35
			10	12	5	$ 27
		M2 Independents	40	50	0	$ 90
			50	10	0	60
			8	10	0	$ 18
	CAN	M3 Major Chains	20	25	15	$ 60
			5	6	5	16
			5	7	2	$ 14
		M4 Independents	15	20	25	$ 60
			4	6	5	15
			3	12	8	$ 23
Product Totals	$Revenue		125	135	70	$ 330
	#Volume		69	37	20	126
	$Profit		26	41	15	$ 82

Figure 9.4 Basic PMC Engine sample with Revenue, Volume and Profit

This basic PMC Engine format makes a powerful decision-making tool to more specifically manage and resolve issues impacting your strategy and business.

Now, all the 12 cells above can't be of equal importance relative to your scarce resources, right? Intuitively we know this.

We need to evaluate relative importance by developing criteria that each of the P-M cells can be fairly, and with data, evaluated against, which is Step 3 in creating your PMC Engine.

Step 3: determine the relative importance of criteria

We develop a short list of four to six weighted (not ranked) criteria that makes visible and common the collective reasons why certain Products and Markets are more important than others.

The criteria I outline are not NEW, UNKNOWN or HARD TO DEVELOP – they are basically the same for any business and are based on the normal discussion executives always use in allocating scarce resources, including:

- what size of sales opportunity is possible?
- how much profit will/can we make?
- does it leverage our competitive advantage?

- what's the volume?
- what about the competition?
- what sales are we getting there now?

The profound difference in doing it this way is it gives the leadership team and company **common criteria to make choices**. Common criteria in action create consistent decision-making and consistency in allocating resources to the most important things. This is focus in action – and focused action by employees in your company will create better financial outcomes.

Many companies today handcuff themselves because their executives use different versions of criteria or metrics (e.g., Gross Margin per cent versus Operation Income) or cherry pick the criteria and the relative importance of the criteria to one another – with no ill intent – to make decisions. This diffuses efforts and diminishes results because decisions being made are not considering the same criteria to evaluate similar alternatives.

Weighting criteria simply follows this thinking:

- Find the most importance criteria and give it a 10=High
- Relative to the 10, weigh the rest from 10–1, recognizing that there can be multiple objectives with the same weighting.

The first-pass iteration usually looks something like what is outlined in Table 9.1.

The result of the commonly developed and viewed set of criteria is a powerful priority-setting tool, as each CELL undergoes the objective scrutiny of how well it performs against the criteria.

Yes, each Product-Market cell in your PMC Engine needs to be evaluated against how it performs against the bundle of factors your team deemed important for the business. A simple decision analysis tool will help make this visible and is outlined in Figure 9.5.

Now you may be thinking, if I have a 5X5 or 6X6 PMC Engine, I have 24 or 36 cells to evaluate; and the answer is, you do. But what's the alternative: your Products and Markets are being evaluated and resourced by some form of ad hoc or multi-version criteria in

Table 9.1 Format to develop and evaluate how each cell in the PMC Engine satisfies criteria important to the business: sample criteria only

Determine the relative emphasis of each product-market cell using the following criteria:

Relative criteria weight (High=10, Low=1)	Criteria What's important to the business?	Metric What do we mean by the criteria?	Target What is the numerical standard or range?
8	Market potential	$MM USD	>10
10	Profit	$ Operating income	>0–20
8	Growth	% per annum	>8–15
10	Competitive advantage	% Gross margin	>20–60
7	Competitive intensity	# of competitors with greater than 15% market share	0–6

1. Determine Relative Emphasis of each Product / Market Cell

2. Score the 12 Product - Market Cells Against the Critiera
(Criteria Weight X Score) - then SUM all the totals for a Final Overall Total

Relative Criteria Weight High=10 Low=1	Criteria What's important to the business	Metric What do we mean by the criteria?	Target What is the numerical standard or range?	Score	P1-M1 Total	Score	P2-M1 Total	Score	P3-M1 Total	Score	P3-M2 Total	Score	P2-M2 Total	No Products sold in this segment	Score	P1-M3 Total	Score	P2-M3 Total	Score	P3-M3 Total	Score	P1-M4 Total	Score	P2-M4 Total	Score	P3-M4 Total
8	Market Potential	$MM USD	>10	10	80	9	72	8	64	10	80	10	80		8	64	10	80	7	56	8	64	7	56	10	80
10	Profit	$ Operating Income	>0-20	9	90	10	100	9	90	9	90	9	90		10	100	9	90	9	90	8	80	8	80	9	90
8	Growth	% per annum	>8-15	8	64	8	64	6	48	7	56	8	64		7	56	7	56	7	56	8	64	7	56	7	56
10	Competitive Advantage	% Gross margin	> 20-60	10	100	8	80	4	40	6	60	4	40		7	70	10	100	5	50	8	80	8	80	9	90
7	Competitive Intensity	# of competitors with greater than 15% of Market share	0-6	10	70	8	56	4	28	7	49	3	21		7	49	8	56	5	35	8	56	6	42	7	49
Step 3. Sum Scores and Stratify CELLs into 3 Groups - High, Med, Low					404		372		270		335		295			339		382		287		344		314		365

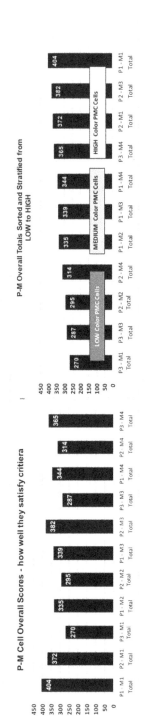

P-M Cell Overall Scores - how well they satisfy critiera

P-M Overall Totals Sorted and Stratified from LOW to HIGH

LOW Color PMC Cells

MEDIUM Color PMC Cells

HIGH Color PMC Cells

Figure 9.5 Full decision matrix example to evaluate and score each P-M cell for relative emphasis and then assign color coding

your organization as you read this book anyway, so why not eliminate the disconnects and use common criteria to set a common decision-making foundation?

In practice, the initial effort is very enlightening to the team and, in our work session, groups usually complete this in no more than 60 minutes. Plus, it highlights the importance and gets alignment on "what do we mean by" profit, growth, market potential and others as the criteria-metrics-target format uncovers misconceptions or diverse views. And these differences in thinking are what your business owners and leaders are using to run the business today.

After scoring them, we want to simplify this and code or color them based on their scoring performance. We stratify them into three categories as outlined in Figure 9.6 and call them:

- **HIGH** – White
- **MEDIUM** – Light grey
- **LOW** – Dark grey
- **NO PRIORITY or NO EXISTING SALES** – Black

Note: ONLY for this book do we use monotone colors – in practice HIGH is GREEN, MEDIUM is YELLOW and LOW is BLUE.

The final output after scoring and color coding each cell is a SIMPLE but very powerful one-page tool we call the **PMC Engine with emphasis**, as shown in Figure 9.7.

The PMC Engine is a visual, dynamic decision-making view of your current Product and Markets – what you sell to who – that represents the current strategic choices (Products to offer and Markets to serve) you have made and the criteria that was used to make those choices.

It is your economic engine. Remember, these are the same Product and Market choices that emerged from the Strategic Assumptions and Implications you developed in Chapter 6.

Because the PMC Engine represents 100 per cent of your Volume, Revenue and EBITDA for your business and, importantly, 100 per cent of where your *scarce* capital, time, people and effort is apportioned, all your issues and opportunities reside in this construct.

There are many other versions or hybrids that can be created – including one that gives the Sales, Volume and Profit per cell as a percentage of totals, as depicted in Figure 9.8.

Now how can we make a PMC Engine even more important and sharper for current and future decision-making?

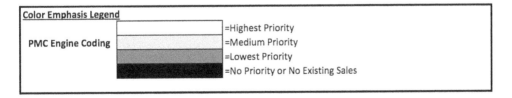

Figure 9.6 PMC coding legend for relative cell emphasis

PMC ENGINE 2017 1 Fiscal Year			1 Year PMC Engine Budgeted Fiscal in Sales of USD$ MM's - Units (000's) and Operating Income			
			Current Products			Market Totals
			P1-Pants	P2-Shirts	P3-Belts	
Current Markets	US	M1 Major Chains	50	40	30	$ 120
			10	15	10	35
			10	12	5	$ 27
		M2 Independents	40	50		$ 90
			50	10		60
			8	10		$ 18
	CAN	M3 Major Chains	20	25	15	$ 60
			5	6	5	16
			5	7	2	$ 14
		M4 Independents	15	20	25	$ 60
			4	6	5	15
			3	12	8	$ 23
Product Totals	$Revenue		125	135	70	$ 330
	#Volume		69	37	20	126
	$Profit		26	41	15	$ 82

Color Emphasis Legend

PMC Engine Coding		=Highest Priority
		=Medium Priority
		=Lowest Priority
		=No Priority or No Existing Sales

Figure 9.7 Fully developed PMC Engine with budgeted financials and coded cells that illustrate relative P-M priorities and where to allocate scarce resources

Fine-tuning a PMC Engine

When most CEOs and leadership teams create (or uncover) their first PMC Engine, they usually share a few common remarks or observations:

- It seems so obvious —product/markets
- I often thought of the business that way
- We don't collect the data relative to products and markets
- This gives a more customer view of our business
- This forces us to apportion versus squander scarce resources to the most important areas
- We don't have the EBITDA data at that level
- We don't collect the data relative to products and markets (not a repeat sentence)

PMC ENGINE 2017 1 Fiscal Year			1 Year PMC Engine - As % of Total Sales, Units and Profit			
			Current Products			Market Totals
			P1-Pants	P2-Shirts	P3-Belts	
Current Markets	US	M1 Major Chains	15%	12%	9%	36%
			8%	12%	8%	28%
			12%	15%	6%	33%
		M2 Independents	12%	15%		27%
			40%	8%		48%
			10%	12%		22%
	CAN	M3 Major Chains	6%	8%	5%	18%
			4%	5%	4%	13%
			6%	9%	2%	17%
		M4 Independents	5%	6%	8%	18%
			3%	5%	4%	12%
			4%	15%	10%	28%
TOTALS	$Revenue		38%	41%	21%	100%
	#Volume		55%	29%	16%	100%
	$Profit		32%	50%	18%	100%

Color Emphasis Legend

PMC Engine Coding
- =Highest Priority
- =Medium Priority
- =Lowest Priority
- =No Priority or No Existing Sales

Figure 9.8 PMC Engine with Sales, Volume and Profit as a percentage of totals

All valid points.

No company has or ever will have perfect data. But the PMC Engine, even as a rough "back of the envelope" version, is a powerful starting point. The key learning is that it makes the Product, Market and Capabilities visible against the backdrop of your understanding of why customers buy and where you make money.

The PMC Engine can be fine-tuned further or customized in the following ways, with each of these variants being seen as an evolution in making it better, not as a barrier to not creating or using one if you don't have the time, resources or data.

You should work with your team and resources to populate each PMC Engine cell with the following INTERNAL data:

1 **BUDGETED versus ACTUAL**: Revenue, Volume and Operating Income should be tracked on a monthly and no later than a quarterly period. A bar or line graph format is recommended.

2   **Strategic Initiatives**: those critical few projects and investments to build or strengthen your competitive advantage.
3   **Opportunity Pipeline**: in $ and units for the calendar year.
4   **Existing versus Future Emphasis for this Cell**: the relative shift in importance this cell will undergo during a one-year time frame that requires efforts to BUILD, MAINTAIN or EXIT, as well as required activities to realize these changes.

Samples of information that can be inserted and formats for PMC Engine cells are illustrated below (Figure 9.9 is just one sample cell).

As stated earlier, waiting for 100 per cent of data is never an option: even if you don't have the "PERFECT NEW REPORT" on market size, put in guesstimates from your team's best thinking or, as a last resort, an NMD (needs more data) placeholder and assign a junior resource to complete the calibration search.

In addition, each cell can be used to capture key external data points that serve as a better filter toward more balanced (i.e., external and internal factors) and insightful decision-making. Consider adding these factors to each cell:

1   **Market Size**: external in units or $ (ideally both)
2   **Market Segment Growth**: in per cent per annum
3   **Competitive Differentiators**: customer purchase criteria or dimensions valued by the buyer and that they pay a premium for
4   **Top Two Competitors**: add the top rivals that your sales force is typically competing with or running into in the market.

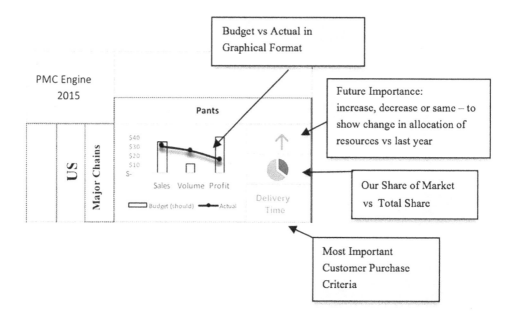

Figure 9.9 Sample PMC Engine with cell data graph format to show SHOULD versus ACTUAL performance and integrate additional Market Intelligence data

These fine-tuning points, as an option to embed in the PMC Engine, provide a more powerful and relevant portrayal, on one page, of the most important Product-Market aspects that the C-Suite executive team needs to use to make dynamic decisions and to keep a watchful eye on.

In practice, the addition of the PMC Engine data takes less time than most companies first believe because the majority of this data already sits somewhere or resides in the head of someone in your organization. The exercise to centralize it into a single powerful decision-making tool gives the PMC Engine purpose, power and practical application that C-Suite executives and P&L owners will quickly appreciate. It also ensures an OUTSIDE-IN view of the world, which guards against group think and absolute belief in tribal knowledge.

As a rule you must create a PMC Engine for each calendar year: it becomes your budget and subsequent years reflect the time frame of the strategy. This format ensures you don't divorce strategy decisions from budgeting.

We often see many companies with separate budgeting, strategic planning and long-range planning (LRP) processes. When they adopt a PMC Engine, they quickly stop this multi-process approach, as they realize it is one process to drive all time aspects for planning: budget, strategy and LRP (see Figures 9.10a and 9.10b).

In addition, the PMC Engine helps answer the following questions that 99 per cent of the CEOs I have worked with recognize to be "must knows" for driving sustainable profitability:

- Do we really know our **Operating Income/EBITDA numbers by Product and Market cell combination**?
- Do we **use this data to drive our decisions** in the boardroom, lunch room and sales room?
- Are we **engraining a Profitability mindset into our culture** rather than a bigger-is-better mentality?
- Do we know **why our customers buy or don't buy from us**? (Not sales team perceptions but third-party surveys that ask them.)
- Are you **setting up and making critical investments** for the future based on sustainable profitability?

The PMC Engine's power to improve the quality of your company's decision-making is best illustrated with the graphic in Figure 9.11, which shows the logic of connecting criteria, priority and emphasis that equate to 100 per cent of allocated efforts.

PMC Application 2: Growth Options

Identify and evaluate future growth options to sharply determine what's next for the business

Every CEO has asked, is asking or will ask: "How do I grow my business?" With the PMC Engine as a pivot point, the choices or at least places to look can be narrowed down to three:

1   **More Core**: further penetration of current products and markets
2   **More Products**: more new Products to the same customers and Markets
3   **More Markets**: same Products to new Customers or geographies.

PMC ENGINE 2017 — 1 Fiscal Year
1 Year PMC Engine Budgeted Fiscal in Sales of USD$ MM's - Units (000's) and Operating Income $

Current Markets			P1-Pants	P2-Shirts	P3-Belts	Market Totals
US	M1 Major Chains	$Revenue	50	40	30	$120
		#Volume	10	15	10	35
		$Profit	10	12	5	27
	M2 Independents	$Revenue	40	50		$90
		#Volume	50	10		60
		$Profit	8	10		18
CAN	M3 Major Chains	$Revenue	20	25	15	$60
		#Volume	5	6	5	16
		$Profit	5	7	2	14
	M4 Independents	$Revenue	15	20	25	$60
		#Volume	4	6	5	15
		$Profit	3	12	8	23
Product Totals		$Revenue	125	135	70	$330
		#Volume	69	37	20	126
		$Profit	26	41	15	82

PMC ENGINE 2018 — 1 Fiscal Year
1 Year PMC Engine Budgeted Fiscal in Sales of USD$ MM's - Units (000's) and Operating Income $

Current Markets			P1-Pants	P2-Shirts	P3-Belts	Market Totals
US	M1 Major Chains	$Revenue	60	50	30	$140
		#Volume	20	15	10	45
		$Profit	10	12	5	27
	M2 Independents	$Revenue	40	50		$90
		#Volume	50	10		60
		$Profit	20	10		30
CAN	M3 Major Chains	$Revenue	40	25	15	$80
		#Volume	5	6	5	16
		$Profit	5	7	2	14
	M4 Independents	$Revenue	15	20	25	$60
		#Volume	4	6	5	15
		$Profit	3	12	8	23
Product Totals		$Revenue	155	145	70	$370
		#Volume	79	37	20	136
		$Profit	38	41	15	94

PMC ENGINE 2019 — 1 Fiscal Year
1 Year PMC Engine Budgeted Fiscal in Sales of USD$ MM's - Units (000's) and Operating Income $

Current Markets			P1-Pants	P2-Shirts	P3-Belts	Market Totals
US	M1 Major Chains	$Revenue	70	50	40	$160
		#Volume	10	15	10	35
		$Profit	30	12	5	47
	M2 Independents	$Revenue	40	50	5	$95
		#Volume	50	10	5	65
		$Profit	8	10	2	20
CAN	M3 Major Chains	$Revenue	40	25	15	$80
		#Volume	5	15	5	25
		$Profit	10	7	2	19
	M4 Independents	$Revenue	15	20	25	$60
		#Volume	4	6	10	20
		$Profit	3	12	8	23
Product Totals		$Revenue	165	145	85	$395
		#Volume	69	46	30	145
		$Profit	51	41	17	109

Figure 9.10a PMC Engine for a company with a strategic time frame of three years: you would create one PMC Engine per fiscal year. Cell colors change as relative emphasis evolves based on the external environment and internal decisions.

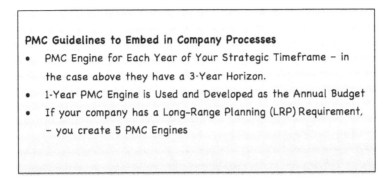

Figure 9.10b Guidelines to effectively embed the PMC Engine in a company

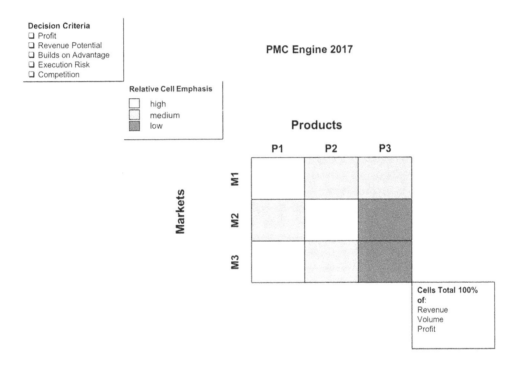

Figure 9.11 Steps showing decision-making rationale behind PMC Engine

To explore growth options, we use the PMC Engine and introduce Igor Ansoff's well-traveled paths for growth thinking, first outlined in a 1957 paper on strategy (see Figure 9.12).

Many companies use the Ansoff Matrix effectively; however, I routinely see four Gaps when this construct is applied that diminishes its effectiveness:

* a lack of visible criteria to evaluate growth paths;
* trying to "grow" in both directions, thinking diversification is a panacea;

		Products	
		Existing	**New**
Markets	**Existing**	**Penetration** (more core)	**Product Development** (more new products)
	New	**Market Development** (more new markets)	**Diversification** (new products and new markets)

Figure 9.12 Ansoff's Paths for Growth Matrix

Source: Ansoff, I.: Strategies for Diversification, *Harvard Business Review*, Vol. 35 Issue 5, Sep–Oct 1957, pp. 113–124

- not having a current baseline complete with financials that represent existing Products and Markets to pivot from; and
- not having a more decomposed view of Products and Market segments with a relative emphasis (as the PMC Engine provides).

To counter these Gaps, I recommend the adaptions shown in Figure 9.13 in concert with the PMC Engine.

1   Set and use criteria to evaluate any NEW Product and/or NEW Market options you are considering.
2   Leverage your SWOT, Strategic Assumptions and Market Intelligence resources to identify realistic PRODUCT or MARKET Opportunities.

As we did earlier, employ the PMC Engine criteria for emphasis to evaluate growth options.

PMC Application 3: Future Key Capabilities

Determine and quantify Key Capabilities that will make your strategy real and realistic, and will provide a base test of the Return on Invested Capital

Key capabilities are the third and final **BIG DECISION** executives are faced with (see Figure 9.14). (Products to offer/not offer and Markets to serve/not serve being Big Decisions 1 and 2, respectively.)

While much has been written on both setting and implementing strategy, in the lion's share of literature, I notice there seems to be a missing link that clearly and practically outlines a one-pager on what the company must change as it goes from its AS IS to SHOULD BE future strategy state.

This misstep leaves the rationale for the vision unchecked or hazy, causing people to question how valid or viable it really is.

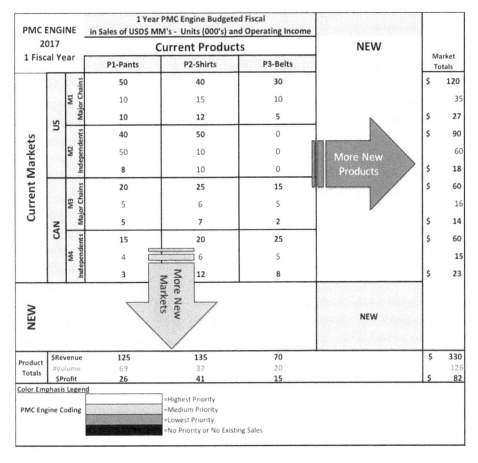

PMC ENGINE 2017 1 Fiscal Year			1 Year PMC Engine Budgeted Fiscal in Sales of USD$ MM's - Units (000's) and Operating Income			NEW	Market Totals
			Current Products				
			P1-Pants	P2-Shirts	P3-Belts		
Current Markets	US	M1 Major Chains	50	40	30		$ 120
			10	15	10		35
			10	12	5		$ 27
		M2 Independents	40	50	0		$ 90
			50	10	0	More New Products	60
			8	10	0		$ 18
	CAN	M3 Major Chains	20	25	15		$ 60
			5	6	5		16
			5	7	2		$ 14
		M4 Independents	15	20	25		$ 60
			4	6	5		15
			3	12	8		$ 23
NEW			More New Markets			NEW	
Product Totals	$Revenue		125	135	70		$ 330
	#Volume		69	37	20		126
	$Profit		26	41	15		$ 82

Color Emphasis Legend

PMC Engine Coding:
= Highest Priority
= Medium Priority
= Lowest Priority
= No Priority or No Existing Sales

Figure 9.13 PMC Engine overlay on Ansoff's Paths for Growth Matrix creates a stronger data–driven decision-making tool to evaluate growth options

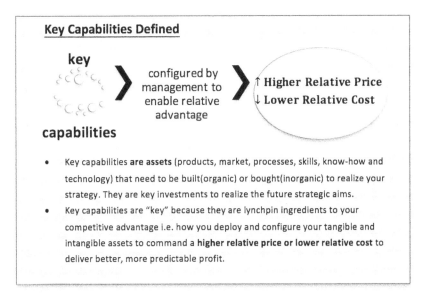

Key Capabilities Defined

key → configured by management to enable relative advantage → ↑ **Higher Relative Price** ↓ **Lower Relative Cost**

capabilities

- Key capabilities **are assets** (products, market, processes, skills, know-how and technology) that need to be built(organic) or bought(inorganic) to realize your strategy. They are key investments to realize the future strategic aims.
- Key capabilities are "key" because they are lynchpin ingredients to your competitive advantage i.e. how you deploy and configure your tangible and intangible assets to command a **higher relative price or lower relative cost** to deliver better, more predictable profit.

Figure 9.14 Key capabilities: bought or built tangible and intangible assets the company configures to offer products to customers that result in higher profit relative to their competitors through a better relative Price or Cost position – this advantage must show up on the Income Statement

What is lacking and what we outline for the CEOs to use is a practical Advantage-Future Capabilities (AFC) Matrix. This matrix is a detailed set of capabilities that must be buttressed, bought, built or phased out relative to each Product-Market segment.

The AFC Matrix is the defining set of specs that details opportunities and investments needed in exchange for the return these CORE and NEW Product and Market cells or mix are expected to produce. In short, it's an initial but meaningful ROIC (Return on Invested Capital) visual that firmly links Product-Market cells to investments relative to the Sales and Profits that the future strategy promises to deliver.

In addition, it is the ultimate one-page guide for board members to see and test just how "REAL" and "REALISTIC" the strategy options being proposed are. The AFC Matrix is a natural extension of the PMC Engine and helps to explain the WHAT, WHY, HOW MUCH and WHEN behind any investments and implementation initiatives being considered.

Put another way, it's the business case that says:

If we envision this purpose and path for our company, across these product and market priorities, then to achieve these goals, we require "X" (the X is future key capabilities).

And these resources must provide an advantage against the competition that produces above-average profitability through higher relative Price and/or lower relative Cost compared to the competition.

I have outlined below the worksheet and three steps to complete your Advantage-Future Capabilities (AFC) Tool in Figure 9.15. Before you begin, **ensure you have clarity on your Product and Market choices** – which your strategy process should avail – as well as meaningful and valid "relative importance" purchasing criteria for your segments.

Three steps to use the AFC Matrix with your executive team

1   **Outline** your high-level current and new Product/Market segments.
2   **Incorporate** relative importance purchasing criteria and select attributes that are most critical for that segment and the competitive advantage.
3   **Populate Advantage-Future Capabilities** for **each Product-Market** segment:
    A   **Quantify potential**
    B   **Define customer criteria and basis of competition**
    C   **Describe the Capability to close the Gap** – the asset to be bolstered, bought or built that delivers the ability to do "X" as an outcome
    D   **Set the Investment and Timing** – when it must be "operational" and will deliver the intended benefits.

Use the template in Figure 9.15 to complete your company's AFC Matrix.

For example, a business case that unfolds from a completed AFC Matrix follows something like what is shown below; it is an early and powerful reality check for your strategy.

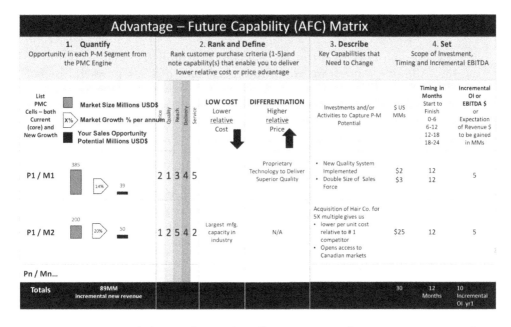

Figure 9.15 AFC Matrix: linking product-market cells to customer purchase criteria, competitive advantage and the change in key capabilities to deliver a higher profit and better ROIC

The simplified (yes . . . simplified to show the thinking) example below illustrates how the Product-Market choices made by fictional Company ABC and represented in the PMC Engine are linked to results required relative to the investments needed to deliver profit:

- **2015 Revenue ACTUALS ➔ $80 million Sales, $10 million OI**

If we invest $30 million in organic and inorganic Capabilities (see Figure 9.15), we will get a one-year incremental change in OI of $10 million.

- **2016 Revenue SHOULD BE ➔ $139 million Sales, $20 million OI**

The ROIC big decision?

Would you invest $30 million to go from a 10 to 20 million OI company per year (an incremental 10 million)? a rough pass of 10 / 30 = 33 per cent ROIC?

A great ROIC average for many companies is 10 per cent! The takeaway from the strategy process and the AFC Matrix is that it forces scrutinization and eventually prioritization of tradeoffs and investments. It makes the strategy real.

No one is selling the farm at this point; but if the front part of your strategy process is robust, it should channel you to a point where this type of analysis is based in reality and provides a starting point to begin to evaluate options, get board sign-off and make plans for implementation.

Now what

A PMC Engine is the central decision-making hub for your economic engine. Aligning your team to common criteria delivers powerful benefits because decision makers use the same parameters to make decisions, track performance and think about the business – which may be lacking now.

Actions:

1   Build a PMC Engine
2   Ensure your team deliberates and agrees on the criteria driving emphasis
3   Incorporate Product by Market financials
4   Build out the PMC variations and Market Intelligence detail as needed
5   Develop the AFC Matrix – define what is needed to realize your strategy.

10 Goals and Gaps

How to find and fixate on the few goals that matter

 After 5pm

Goals have three practical aims in strategy:

1 **Force focus**
2 **Enable accountability**
3 **Facilitate finding cause of performance gaps**

Too many strategies suffer from ambiguous or overreaching goals. Poor goals drive diffused actions and create confusion as they cascade down the organization.

A company should have no more than three above-all-else goals to focus their resources. These goals come directly from the framework of strategy – namely, a Product or Market Goal, a Capability to drive a future advantage Goal and a Financial Goal.

As CEO, the acid test is: if you achieve only these three goals during the fiscal year, your board should applaud you and you can be confident you are moving your organization in the right strategic direction.

Goal and Gaps is the third and last pillar to build the strategy system which included: 1. Strategic Assumption; and 2. PMC Engine.

Earlier we defined strategy as the set of choices – **Products, Markets and Capabilities** – that determine the purpose and path of your company. Given this common definition, I can provide clear guidance on and debunk some all-too-prevalent myths about setting strategic goals.

At the end of the day, we need strategic goals for three reasons:

1 Focus on the few things that matter
2 Make people accountable
3 Find out why we are hitting the mark or coming up short

These are three straightforward aims that seem to have gotten lost in many organizations. Whether it has been due to mainstream books, self-appointed gurus or "bigger has to be better" thinking, we can't be sure. Before we speak to the rationale and benefits of goals, let's look at some of the pitfalls we see in organizations when they set goals.

There are five main culprits I encounter when working with clients in setting strategic goals. I recommend you to check your organization against these and fix them.

Culprit #1: must be long term

A culprit that needs resetting for the benefit of your organization is that strategic goals need to be described as long term. Over the years when I've asked a CEO or leadership team to define strategy and therefore the goals associated with it, the first answer is usually, "strategic goals must be long term."

My response is: what is long term anyways?

- **10 years?**
- **20 years?**
- **3 years?**
- **5 years?**
- **1 year?**

Usually the group settles collectively on a safe five years as long term.

A strategic goal need not be long term (whatever your definition of "long" is). A strategic goal is one that achieves the **Product, Market or Capabilities** choices the company made when they developed their strategy.

Strategic goals are born out of the dynamics of the industry, competition, substitutes, technology and the macro forces in the world in which we live. They represent your choices based on the nature of your industry balanced against the purpose and path the leadership of your company determines and what is realistic.

It's true that many goals are long term – greater than a 12-month effort – because the nature of turning an organization around or achieving major shifts in resources takes time, or developing a new product requires a set cycle to design and launch; but the reason for "long term" is the nature of the Products, Markets and Capabilities required against the backdrop of the industry you reside in.

The other danger of associating strategic goals with "long term" is that it creates a false sense of NON-URGENCY in the company. If you look at Google, Uber, Facebook or Amazon right now, they have strategic goals being accomplished in days and months, not years. This is primarily because technology, customer feedback and expectation cycles have shortened to such as level that it's impossible to say what their strategy aims are in 5 or 10 years. It's not that they don't have longer term missions – part vision, part market – but they are responding to what's working now.

The simple takeaway is: strategic goals should not be assumed as long term only – there are reasons behind the distance a company looks out and goals it sets; not clarifying this handcuffs your organization.

Culprit #2: too many goals

By now many, many CEOs and leaders have recognized that more is not better. It might sound interesting to have eight strategic goals – but the reality is the company, its leaders and its employees, not to mention its board, just get lost in all those goals.

There should be no more than three strategic goals per fiscal year.

This means if you have more than three – even if they are "good ones" – you should reexamine your strategy and ask what are the fundamental outcomes that, if achieved, represent the most important strategic aims of the business.

By avoiding too many goals, you will find many of those mission-critical initiatives in your implementation portfolio eliminated and scarce resources that were stretched thin are now purposefully assigned to projects that matter.

Culprit #3: having stretch or Big Hairy Audacious Goals (BHAG)

Stretch and Big Hairy Audacious Goals (BHAG) seem to have waned over the last three years. They used to be the normal language we heard in companies. Stretch means "we have a budget but we bump it up to a higher number" and BHAG . . . I think the acronym explains itself.

Both of these represent a type of thinking I believe undermines the intelligence and integrity of the people in the organization. Setting false or unrealistic goals does nothing to move the organization forward. If anything, it's a partial cause of lack of accountability or people not wanting to sign up and own their piece of performance.

The process of setting strategic goals remains the same: they should be realistic, understood by the organization, set with integrity and achievable. They should be set based on leadership's belief in what their company wants to become and what exploits their competitive advantage.

If you engage people in the thinking to create strategic goals, you will get better goals and more commitment than you can by crafting (and trying to manage) some artificial, super aspirational, motivational number that people know they can't meet or has not been set by sound thinking based on relevant external and internal data.

Over time you set up an organization that has the chosen few hitting numbers, the critical many despondent and a leadership team wondering why no one is on the same page.

Culprit #4: ambiguous goals

Too often we see a presentation slide that lists strategic goals such as these that I recently noticed:

For 2016 our goals are to

1   Be number 1 in the market
2   Have the highest quality products
3   Be the leader in customer service
4   Gain share

These seem simple enough, but when I asked the leadership team how they were set, what they meant and how they were measured, some of them came back quickly with the answer that number 1 in the market was expressed in the value of Sales, while others thought this was in terms of share value and, still others, brand recognition. No agreement from the leadership team.

"The highest quality products" was in response to last year's recall of products and "customer service" was the differentiator attributed to get our price premium. Still no alignment on common metrics that people tracked and tested.

Goals need specificity – ambiguous goals cause frustration. This culprit needs to be addressed in your organization, as it again fuels lack of accountability and ownership.

Culprit #5: not understood or relatable to all employees

If you want to engage your workforce, ensure the goals are meaningful to all your employees no matter what the pay grade. Too often CEOs and leadership teams set goals that cut a divide between themselves and the organization.

For example, one company I saw set their goals as:

• Free Cash Flow 2X Prior Year
• Earnings Per Share (EPS) to have a 10 Basis Points Gain
• Top Line Growth to be 50 per cent from Acquisitions with minimal new Debt

While the intent to the board, leadership team and Wall Street analysts may resonate, how can the average manager and leader see themselves and their jobs in those goals, be motivated and/or drive behavior on a daily basis to achieve them?

They can't. Goals like this alienate the very workforce that you are seeking to engage.

Strategic goals need to be set in straightforward language that all employees can see themselves contributing to – or that they can come to understand how they fit in. If you don't have goals that people understand, you should reset and communicate them differently. Your employees will thank you.

Strategically meaningful goals ensure everyone in the organization can answer the question: "Above all else, what are the two or three things that define success for our business this year?"

So where do good strategic goals come from?

Finding and setting strategic goals

Strategic goals mirror and define the very definition of strategy. As companies work through the two pillars of setting strategy – defining their Strategic Assumptions and building a PMC Engine that explains their products to offer, markets to serve, capabilities to build, and path for growth – they see the future benchmarks that represent what they must become.

Good, sound and practical strategic goals follow these categories:

1 **Emphasis on Profit**: OI (operating income), Free Cash Flow (FCF) or EBITDA metrics for profit are good starting points. The emphasis on profit ties to our belief and experience with clients that if you are not making money that can be reinvested and/or distributed to shareholders, why are you in business? Strategic goals can also include a Revenue target, as everyone can relate to it and recognize that the Revenue minus Cost (RCP model) gets us back to profit, as outlined in Chapter 5.
2 **Product or Market**: As we discussed earlier in this chapter, there really are two fundamental paths for growth – sell more products or sell to more markets. Depending on the path your company selects, you will have one strategic goal that represents your aim for growth. Here the metrics may be Revenue, new product introductions or new customer deals acquired as examples.

3 **Key Capability**: This is the other category for which you need a strategic goal. Key Capabilities are those competencies, skills and processes that drive competitive advantage – or will drive advantage for your business in the future. To keep your premium or low-cost position relative to the competition, you need competencies to emerge that most likely support the PRODUCT or MARKET path for growth and deliver the PROFIT. Key capabilities are the lynchpin for investing in the business that supports the other two goals.

You might be thinking: this is super intuitive or seems way too clean and simple to be right, repeatable and sound for all companies.

But it is true. In over 17 years of working and facilitating strategies for clients, PROFIT, PRODUCTS or MARKETS, and KEY CAPABILITIES always emerge as the three natural choices that made sense and provided meaningful focus for the company and its employees.

This simple rationale for setting strategic goals relieved many CEOs and leadership teams because it built in checkpoints that ensured the elements in their strategy fit together from top to bottom. There was no more "shoot from the hip," "drive in" and "I just thought of it, wow we should be this big" goals. Goals were rooted in sound strategic thinking.

What is more, by using this format to set strategic goals, your organization will naturally eliminate or sharply lessen the five culprits that were set out at the beginning of the chapter that derail organizational focus:

1 Naturally Long Term
2 Too Many
3 Stretch or BHAG
4 Ambiguous
5 Not Understood or Relatable

Here is a format that you can use to audit and/or set new goals with your leadership team. Note these are sample goals; the key thing is to follow the format in Table 10.1.

Figure 10.1 shows a sanitized client example that was published each quarter and visible to all employees.

The last critical point on having strategic goals set for the year – the SHOULD (or Budget), as we call it – sets up an accountable, traceable system that you can use as the starting point to find root cause from.

Table 10.1 Format and sample of three strategic goals for a fiscal year: depending on the path for growth, a company would select either the Product or Market Goal – not both

Strategic category	Goal	Metric	Target	Data source
1 PROFIT	Operating Income	$ in MMs	100	CFO Report
2A PRODUCT (if your path for growth is new products to the same markets)	Revenue from New Products	$ MMs	10	Sales X Report
2B MARKET (if your path for growth is same product to new markets)	New Revenue China	$ MMs	5MM	Sales Y Report
3 Key Capabilities (investment to drive advantage)	New Products Commercialized	# per year	4	NPD Report

IV. Focus Goal Results – Year-to-Date October 2015

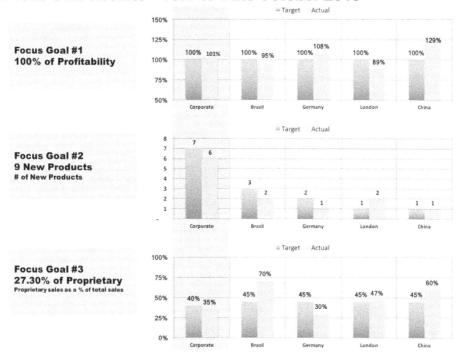

Figure 10.1 Strategic goals: sanitized client example. This example illustrates total company performance fixated on Profitability, New Products and Proprietary sales. Additionally, the focus goals are stratified by global BU performance to further drill down on accountability.

Finding cause – the positive or negative variances along the way – forces the organization to actually use their strategy because the Strategic Assumptions and Implications that underpin the rationale for growth and choices you make on Products and Markets are tied into the three goals that you need to track. It's the data that validates your thinking and gives you the proactive position to lead your business.

Meaningful data and well-designed metrics enable you to use your strategy. The one-off retreat to set and forget your strategy goes away. Your company takes an important step in becoming a strategic-thinking and decision-making company.

Let's end this discussion on goals with a few comments and caveats that will answer typical questions that arise when setting goals:

1 *How do these goals fit into the Strategic Performance Indicators covered in Chapter 5?*
   The eight indicators I covered in Chapter 5 (under the categories FINANCIAL, CUSTOMER, PROCESS and PEOPLE) encapsulate the strategic goals.

2 *How do we get people to own these goals when they are so strategic?*
   Ownership begins with understanding and by using the format laid out – people can all understand the Product, Market and Capabilities aspects of the business. They can easily understand how their role directly or indirectly relates to the

fundamental dimensions of strategy. In addition, by explaining where profit comes from – Revenue minus Cost – they quickly see, be they manager or production line worker or in sales or finance, that their roles go into demand generation for the R or they have a part in the C (operations, creation of products and support for customers).

3   *What if our company already uses the SMART method to set goals?*
The Specific, Measurable, Actionable, Realistic and Timely (SMART) label is used in many organizations for goal setting. It provides a sound starting point. You might additionally consider using my new SMART acronym in your organization for setting sound and achievable strategic goals:
  • **Strategic**: if it contains PMC dimensions
  • **Minimal**: no more than three
  • **Available**: understood by all and all can contribute to it
  • **Real**: no stretch or BHAGs
  • **Tied to Profit**: ensure Profitability is a focus

 Now what

Ensure you have no more than three strategic goals that fall into these three buckets:

  • **PROFIT**
  • **PRODUCT or MARKET**
  • **KEY CAPABILITIES**

1   Use the goal, metric, target and data source format to set them. Get your leadership team to double-check them against the SMART criteria.
2   Remember these goals define success for a one-year period and should be made visual to the entire organization.
3   When tracking performance, remember you are looking for both positive and negative variances (Gaps, deviations) that you must not just report on, but find root cause for.

This simple yet powerful exercise – as a starting point to make your organization more focused, accountable and able to track true strategic achievement – will simplify and unclutter the conflicting voices and directions the organization may be pulling itself and its scarce resources in today.

Part III

USE

How to use your strategy to drive results

11 Introduction to using the TDG System

How to practically use the tools, get the most from your team and deliver business results

 After 5pm

With the barriers blocking strategy removed and the three pillars (Assumptions, PMC ENGINE and GOALS and GAPS) of the Strategy System created, we have SIMPLIFIED greatly your ability to set and remove barriers impacting strategy in your company.

It's time to fulfill the last part of the promise that was written on the cover of this book: getting your executives and managers to use the strategy. To use it they must be able to:

- Test your strategy: seven CEO punchlist criteria to evaluate your plan
- Check in quarterly: finding IF and WHY your strategy is working
- Reinstate root cause: cause is king for sustaining results

These last three areas set up your organization to USE their strategy because they make use of the three pillars. They use the tools that defined the purpose and path of the company to evaluate its strength, set a regular cadence to evaluate performance and strategic thinking and finally reinstate root cause by looking at the POSITIVE and NEGATIVE variations that occur in the focus goals, Strategic Performance Indicators and PMC Engine. Simple.

In **Part 1, FIX**, we outlined six Gaps limiting strategy:

- **The absence of shared language**: why no one is on the same page
- **Mistaken identity**: strategy is a decision-making process, not an event
- **Outsourcing strategy**: don't bypass sweat equity
- **Forgetting about profit**: why is there no vice president of profitability?
- **Mixed up on metrics**: when was the answer ever "have more metrics"?
- **Vague Latitude**: assumed buy-in from boards to employees

In **Part 2, BUILD**, three pillars formed the strategy system and provided the bare necessities to develop a pragmatic but powerful strategy and usable decision-making tools for your organization. These pillars are shown in Table 11.1.

Table 11.1 Three pillars and intent of TDG Strategy System

Pillar	Purpose
1 Strategic Assumptions	Connect outside to inside
2 PMC Engine	Criteria-driven priorities to drive investments and profitability
3 Goals and Gaps	Properly set and fixate the company on the few important goals

In Part 3, USE, we cover three critical pieces that enable your organization to have confidence in its strategy that the goals set can be achieved, they can put the system into play and they build the sought-after executive and CEO truism that mid-course corrections need to be made as a strategy is implemented.

Chapter 12: test your strategy

Upon completion of setting strategy, there is often a great sense of relief . . . and then dread. Relief because the time, sweat equity, analytics and team building that naturally flows from a combined effort is over.

Dread because they realize they have not implemented or achieved any results with the new strategy. At this point in the process, teams are wed to their efforts but still require a "sense-checking" of their strategy and need to critically test alternatives and paths for growth before making the final choice. Chapter 12 provides an evaluation framework to pressure test and select or present the most balanced option(s).

Chapter 13: reinstate root cause

In this penultimate chapter, I outline the simple truths to great strategic performance that we have seen in countless clients. They are adept at reinstating root cause into their executive teams' behavior in a systematic way.

This approach forces them to look at both the POSITIVE and NEGATIVE variations relative to their strategic and financial performance – a root cause process that takes them away from emotional debates and assuming why sales are up or down, removes guesswork and excuses from their lexicon, and focuses them on the search for truth or the factual data that represents what is really happening. This approach encourages the organization to go back to the fundamentals of problem-solving and decision-making to support sustainable EBITDA.

Chapter 14: check in quarterly

The final chapter sets up a recommended scheduling format for the CEO and leadership team to use the tools and map the progress that has been made on the strategy to see IF and WHY it is working (or not working).

Rather than just asking vague questions or re-presenting the strategy that was set, they actually incorporate issues from the organization and learn a system and framework to quickly separate strategic versus operational issues that could otherwise block the achievement of the focus goals.

They can also see how to use Strategic Performance Indicators and, if needed, drill down on the positive and negative deviations in Revenue, Volume and Profit in a very detailed way using the SHOULD versus ACTUAL financials that are now flowing through in the PMC Engine.

Finally, we outline how to build and capture relevant Market Intelligence that can now be integrated into Quarterly Reviews and eliminate the call to buy the big report on the Market or competition, or to invest in the state-of-the-art competitive intelligence software.

 Now what

Ensure you Read Part I and remove the barriers possibly blocking your strategy. Build the strategy system as outlined by the Strategic Assumptions, PMC Engine and Goals and Gaps.

Read Chapters 12–14 to become an executive practitioner and even more valued executive who has a transportable set of strategic tools that you can use in your career to set strategy and realize better financial outcomes.

Find ways to integrate these tools into your organization to drive better financial outcomes and build strategic-thinking leaders in your company.

12 Test your strategy

Seven CEO punchlist criteria that need to be considered

 After 5pm

There is much effort and energy that goes into setting strategy. The synthesis and insights that emerge from the strategy process end up defining the purpose and path for your organization. This output is the ultimate responsibility and privilege for any executive who participates.

Those strategic choices need to be tested and evaluated against set criteria that factor in both external and internal perspectives, back cast to the Strategic Latitude set by the board and consider the risk profile or appetite of your shareholders.

This chapter equips you with tools to test the soundness of your strategy alternatives and set the way forward. Seven criteria are outlined in this chapter to pressure test your strategy before putting it into action.

Business environments are dynamic and will continue to be. There are too many moving forces externally and internally to have confidence to say that the strategy we set is 100 per cent correct – even after months of dedicated efforts.

We know that No Strategy ever devised is 100 per cent correct.

However, to give your firm a higher batting average in delivering on your strategy, you need to test it systematically when it's being developed and check on it quarterly as progress is made.

Any CEO or business leader – no matter what formula or process they use to develop their next strategic path – should evaluate it against these seven critical criteria and questions to avoid becoming short sighted and endorsing one path forward over another.

These seven criteria can be used by any CEO to sense-check their strategy and, importantly, make their thinking and appetite for risk visible to ensure they have covered the bases they want covered, their executive team can weigh in and, importantly, it can pass shareholder and board approval. Let us start by looking at each of the criteria that make up the sense-checking evaluation.

Seven criteria and supporting questions to test strategic alternative(s)

1 Confidence in data

Every company we work with runs up against this challenge: how confident are we in our data (e.g., market size, growth rates, technology trends, raw materials)? There are some executives who want certainty measured in decimal points and others are okay with anecdotal information corralled from the sales force.

The answer lies somewhere in between and the critical step is not to homogenize your comments on data confidence. You need to be specific as to what level of data confidence is being attached to which Products, Markets and Capabilities within the strategy process and be willing to blend judgment with the inherent appetite for risk your company holds. The key piece is to make these decisions and risks (Probability X, the Impact) visible so the leadership team and in many cases the board can effectively weigh in on it.

- **What level of confidence do we have in our data?**

2 Board approval

Importantly, any new strategy will need the support and approval of the company's governing board. From their perspective, such a strategic alternative will need to generate a significant financial return based on data.

A well-thought-out strategy should visibly explain how you will exploit or mitigate external opportunities and threats to achieve board expectations (e.g., financial returns, ROIC thresholds). Remember, long-winded PowerPoint presentations usually create more questions than answers for boards.

- **Will this new strategy gain board approval?**

3 Industry dynamics

C-Suite executives need to identify those vital few industry trends that impact the SUPPLY and DEMAND curves (read: Profitability), and importantly draw quantified implications and actions that their company exercises against them.

In practice, companies usually have a long list of trends they never link or make actionable in their strategy. Alternatively they leave all of the industry insights in the heads of their executives – rendering them useless or susceptible to a debate on alternatives in executive meetings, which is futile.

In practice, when executives collaborate and collaboratively dial in on the industry, they find no more than five to eight critical trends emerging that they must monitor and configure to their company in order to ensure a robust and competitive strategy.

Any more and either they don't have a coherent strategy or they rely on internal folklore and legends that persist in the organization to make unsound, or less than effective, decisions.

- **Does your strategy have five to eight external assumptions that drive quantified internal decision-making and investments?**

4   *Cultural shift*

Is the change too great given the nature of your current culture during the defined time frame? When companies embark on revisiting their strategy, there is usually a wide range of opportunities they can pursue – from evolutionary to revolutionary changes.

The revolutionary strategy on paper may look good, but given the existing processes, leadership competencies and people that exist today, the leap to the future state may be too much to bite off and will backfire – no matter how good the CEO communication email is. The CEO has to consider both sides, and this criteria and question helps check that balance.

- **Does your strategy back-cast against the culture of the organization to determine if it can make the leap?**

5   *Strategic fit*

Is the nature and direction of the Product and Market choices deliberate and coherent? More often than not, companies offer too many products or serve too many markets, or both. Coupled with this is the lack of analytics that tell them true profitability beyond the Gross Profit line – which can be strategically misleading and financially a disaster.

This proliferation of efforts, resources and time trying to satisfy everyone is a critical strategy downfall. The solution is to outline clearly the specific criteria that determine the strategic fit for all the products in a company's portfolio and the markets it serves, and then cascade them down into the organization to empower and align those who actually create the value and do the work in the organization.

Most misalignment in companies occurs because executives and employees are not working from the same priority playbook – which translates into using different criteria (e.g., Customer service rates, Profitability as a priority while Sales focuses on Revenue Growth) to drive decision-making.

- **Does your strategy clearly outline common criteria to set relative priority on which products to offer (or not offer), which markets/customers to serve (or not serve) and which investments in new capabilities will drive superior and sustainable profitability?**

6   *Financial impact*

A strategy's success is measured by the achievement (or not) of its strategic goals. The most important goals focus on financial impact as measured by sustainable profitability (e.g., EBITDA or return on invested capital).

This ensures that a company creates value (cash) that can be invested back into the business and/or paid to the shareholders. Many companies take great pains to articulate and wordsmith strategic visions and missions without setting clear, quantified and realistic financials goals that prove a true competitive advantage exists (i.e., sustainable EBITDA or cash in the bank and resident on the P&L statement).

- **Are your goals strategic? Do they follow the SMART dimensions?**

7 Overall risk *(Probability X Impact=Risk)*

Are we willing to accept the overall Probability of success and the resulting impact of this new path? Many organizations espouse risk management and mitigation, but few in practice subject their strategic plan alternatives to a robust risk analysis.

Every strategy has risk, but the individual risk appetite of the leaders and owners determines the way to proceed, and having a process to evaluate strategic alternatives builds in a deeper commitment to the soundness of the thinking that went into it. Any risk process must not just stop at identifying potential problems, but go further, ask deeper, and link likely reasons and preventative and contingent questions.

Make sure you subject your strategic plan to a proven risk process that goes beyond pointing out areas of concern. Check that it mirrors the risk appetite or profile of yourself as a CEO and the controlling shareholders.

How to apply the seven criteria to sense-check your strategy

You can robustly test your current strategy and potential strategic alternatives using the criteria discussed and outlined in Figure 12.1 by following three steps:

1 **Weight** the seven criteria (10=high, 1=low) relative to how you view the importance of each.
2 **Evaluate** each strategic alternative and score them relative to how well they satisfy *each of the criteria* (10=high, 1=low in terms of how well the alternatives perform in relation to the criteria).
   ★Note that this is the same decision-making method defined in Chapter 9, on setting relative priority for Product-Market cells in the PMC Engine.
3 **Multiply** the criteria weight by the Score for each of the alternatives and total the scores. Any percentage below 75 per cent of the perfect score could be immediately eliminated and/or require a deeper dive to figure out why the Gaps exist in your strategic alternatives and what you can do to resolve them. The score means that the individual or team has only met 75 per cent of the critical criteria that tell them how robust (valid and viable) their strategy is.

Alternatively, involve your strategic leadership team and invite them to score and weight the process independently. You may be surprised by the level of alignment you have.

In any case, you now have a roadmap to guide improvements in your strategic alternatives and are using data-driven decision-making versus politics as your strategy-evaluation approach.

Remember, even in volatile times, you and your competition are facing the same economic and environment factors. Global events are not singling out only your company.

Companies that are growing profitably during uncertain times are doing so by sense-checking their strategies against robust criteria rather than talking themselves into a mindset that their chosen course is correct.

1. Determine and Test Strategic Plan Options			2.Evaluation of Alternatives - Score Options Against the Critiera (Criteria Weight X Score) - then SUM all the totals for a Final Overall Total								
Relative Criteria Weight High=10 Low=1 Criteria	Criteria	Metric What do we mean by the criteria?	Data that supports your score	Score	Alternative 1 New Markets Strategy - Enter China	Data that supports your score	Score	Alternative 2 New Products Strategy - Next Gen Product Line	Score	Alternative N. Data that supports your score	Other Options...
7	Confidence in Data	Do we have confidence in the data to directionally make the decision and proceed with next steps	50% confidence in market data	5	35	75% confidence in market data	10	70	0		0
8	Industry Dynamics	Does it exploit /mitigate industry trends and competitive responses?	Exploits key China competitor trend	9	72	customers looking for new drone technology	10	80	0		0
7	Cultural Shift	Is the change too great given our current culture – during this time frame	No experience to go global	4	28	leverages current innovative culture	8	56	0		0
10	Strategic Fit	Do we build upon and create capabilities to defend and differentiate (price premium) us against the competition?	Commodity Business - eroding margins	4	40	we have pricing power	8	80	0		0
9	Financial Impact	Can we maximize sustained profitable growth during our timeframe?	Unsure of EBITDA in longer horizon	8	72	Business case ROIC and EBITDA clear	10	90	0		0
7	Overall Risk	Are we willing to accept the overall Probability of Success and Resulting Impact of this alternative	Too many unknowns	4	28	Plays to strengths, leverages customer trends	8	56	0		0
10	SLT Ownership	Does this alternative resolve / address the strategic requirements the leadership team defined at the start of the project?	Address Main issues but out of team expertise	7	70	Address Main issues for clear path for gowth	8	80	0		0
58	Perfect Score for a strategic alternative is 58 X 10 if every alternative scored a 10=580				59%			88%			0%
					345 Total			512 Total			0 Total

Figure 12.1 Template and sample criteria to evaluate your current strategy and new options for consideration

◇ **Now what**

Gather your stakeholders and in some cases even board members to collectively evaluate your current strategy versus options being considered.
   Actions to evelute strategic alternatives:

1   Start with the seven criteria outlined
2   Add additional ones as needed
3   Evaluate the alternatives
4   As CEO, make the most balanced decision.

Remember – no strategy is ever **100% right**; that's why you need to use it to make decisions and test thinking to make course corrections.

13 Reinstate root cause

Cause is king for sustaining results

 After 5pm

Root cause needs to be reissued to executive and leadership teams as a *must-have competency*.

The ability, in a systematic way, to find the WHY behind the positive and negative variances in all aspects of the business is a fundamental necessity for sustainable and profitable growth.

Yet this tool seems to have lost its spot in the C-Suite. Problem-solving and decision-making are fundamental tools of the best performing executive teams we work with. They stick with the basics.

Figure 13.1 shows the most powerful performance graphic I have ever seen used by companies who continue to outperform their peers.

Why, you ask?

This graph illustrates a gap in performance. In this case I have highlighted that we should be looking with equal importance at both the good and bad that has occurred and asking WHY? in a structured and critical way.

In many organizations we see that at best they ask WHY for negative variances but overlook asking WHY for the positive variances. These companies are only looking at 50 percent of what's in their wheelhouse to improve performance. And much of the root-cause thinking or tools we see at the executive level are either dusty or dismal in terms of a systematic and common tool for finding cause.

Think about your own organization for a minute. When the numbers indicate that the East is up 35 per cent on operating income but the West, South and North are down -5 per cent, -17 per cent and -22 per cent, respectively, where does the conversation lead?

Maybe the leader team conversation looks something like this:

- What is the North VP doing to deliver such abysmal results?
- What type of leadership is behind those numbers (this is the third month in a row that they have indicated such a dramatic variance)?
- What explanation do you have to be off your budget so dramatically? And don't tell us it seasonal as it's seasonal for the competition as well!

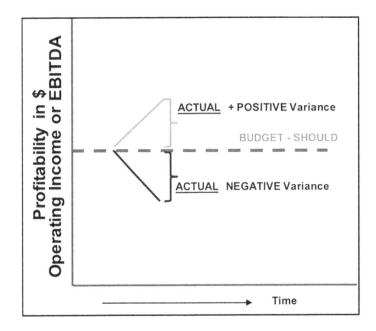

Figure 13.1 The most powerful graphic ever! SHOULD versus ACTUAL performance graph

By the time Mr. North finishes explaining or providing "reasons" to dispel the wrath, the attention turns to Mr. South and Mrs. West for the same drilling.

The meeting ends, the CEO looks at the super performer Mr. East and says, "Well done – dinner is on me!"

This may be an over-simplification but this form of performance evaluation on strategy and financial results is repeated across companies and it needs to be changed. This is surface bumping of performance, not finding the root cause behind positive and negative Gaps and then taking focused action to mitigate, eliminate or exploit the reasons.

So what should we do about this?

We need to reinstate root cause – this means you establish an executive team routine to look at both positive and negative variances and apply a common process for finding cause.

Many executives I have seen in meetings over the years ask WHY sales are down, but seldom have a common process they can point to and use to get down to the proven cause. Allow me to share some background that sets the context of our discussion on root cause.

The co-founder of Thinking Dimensions Global – the company I work for and am CEO of today – was Dr. Charles (Chuck) Kepner (see Figure 13.2). I had the privilege of learning and working with him for over 10 years.

Chuck Kepner had an immeasurable influence and far-reaching impact on corporate problem-solving and decision-making, both nationally and on the global stage over the last 50 years.

His work and methodologies on problem-solving have been applied everywhere from NASA and the CIA to prominent organizations throughout the world.

Figure 13.2 Dr. Charles Kepner (1922–2016), co-founder of Thinking Dimensions Global

Chuck's methods were instrumental in the famed rescue mission of Apollo 13's doomed astronauts and later he collaborated with Dr. Mat-Thys Fourie to develop the next-generation KEPNERandFOURIE method of critical thinking that is used worldwide today.

Contrary to popular thinking, and what I see today in the global clients we work with, Chuck believed that decision-making and problem-solving weren't skills that you either had or you didn't have. Instead, they were tools that could be refined and developed through proper training, dedication and hard work.

Why root-cause analysis has waned in the C–Suite

Because of my background and being part of a company with a pedigree of problem-solving, I suggest five reasons for why the systematic use of root cause has waned at the C–Suite level.

1   *Already trained*

Over the last 50 years globally (and particularly in the United States) there has been a large number of executives who were exposed to some form of root-cause analysis as they were working their way up the corporate ladder.

Whether this was our own KEPNERandFOURIE CauseWise © or the 5 WHYs, it doesn't matter. Executives, once trained, tick the particular box but rarely if ever go back to it and those who never learn a method believe that experience and judgment are all they need to find root cause to performance problems.

2   *Only for the shop floor*

I have noticed a particular phenomenon that seems to spring from the first reason. Those senior executives who have been trained in root cause tend to fall into the trap of assuming that it is purely an operation tool, not something you can apply to intangibles or big-picture strategic issues such as competition, PMC Engine cell performance or why profitability is higher in China than the United States for their organization.

They seem to have positioned root-cause analysis, in their own minds, as relevant for the manufacturing guys along with techniques such as Six Sigma. Executive review sessions and quarterly reviews seem to leave the root-cause technique behind.

3   *Too tool focused*

The reality of using the root-cause tools or in fact any management template is the tools sometimes take center stage rather than the outcomes they are supposed to produce. It's often the case when people learn and are motivated to use a new tool that they end up talking about the tool and the format rather than focusing on the outcomes. You need to ensure the tools are just vehicles to collect, sort and organize relevant information – otherwise the interest of the executive suite will quickly wane or the board will become frustrated.

4   *Rewarded for crisis management or firefighting*

During a recent executive leadership session with a client, our discussion was abruptly stopped when it became known that their most important pharma customer (by Sales and Profit) was receiving substandard product and was threatening to change suppliers.

The team quickly remarked that they are known for their firefighting and this was another opportunity to satisfy the customer. Everyone bands together and they take interim actions to appease the customer, they wrestle with every possible angle of the cause and leave no set of data points unturned.

Given the size of the organization in question and the impact of this particular customer problem (in the 10 millions), I asked if they had a systematic process or common tool that people used. No, came the answer – we are all just good at firefighting as if it were a company badge of honor. This happens more frequently that we think because people fight for a common goal regardless of whether there is a faster, more repeatable way to its achievement.

I remarked to the group that they needed to move from crisis competencies to profit competencies, which captured the CEO's attention and got them thinking: maybe we should reinstate root cause as the standard for the evaluating performance.

5   *Executive resistance*

As strange as it may seem, some executives like the answer they have been giving over the years on why performance is up –and/or down. When root cause is implemented, it can cause discomfort for those who either don't want performance shortfalls to be laid bare or are unenthusiastic about the idea or effort of thinking deeper and really getting to the cause.

These reasons seem to have prevented the adoption of root cause as a **Go-to Tool for executives**.

So why get better at finding cause of negative and positive variations in your strategic performance?

Let us turn to five benefits companies accrue when they re-establish root cause at the executive level:

1 **More speed**

Issues affecting performance are more quickly resolved because there is less fruitless discussion and fewer red herrings to follow or irrelevant data to collect.

2 **Proactive**

Setting the expectation that monthly or quarterly review sessions is about finding the cause, not just presenting the problem, shifts the organization to more proactively search for the right information and better discussions on cause rather than jumping to cause.

3 **Uncover more Profit**

Using a common root-cause process at the executive level increases profit. Why? Rather than just coalescing around what's not working, the conversation is about positive and negative deviations, which doubles the efforts and areas that can be resolved or exploited to raise performance. This two-pronged attack on Profitability delivers higher profit performance.

4 **Data driven**

The thing about root-cause analysis and our decision-making tools is that the focus is on factual data rather than speculation.

The use of the tools quickly ferrets out folklore thinking that has been accepted as fact and uncovers any political plays that support causes that are not based on data – it's a lonely place to hide when you are defending a cause for a problem in your region or business unit for which the data does not support what you are saying.

5 **Simplicity**

Simplicity is the final benefit C-Suite executives receive when root cause is reinstated. Simplicity in this case means returning their focus to the fundamentals that business performance rests on: finding cause, making decisions and mitigating risks. These basic thinking patterns will never be overridden by a "flavor of the month" tool.

So how can my company get better at finding cause of negative and positive variations in our strategic performance?

If your company wants to reinstate root cause, ensure any process that you select and adopt for your company contains these four dimensions:

1 Provide a statement of positive or negative variance

Stating the problem with specificity is one of the most important aspects in root cause. Simply saying "Sales are down" is not a very good problem statement – it's too general. Any problem-solving methodology worth its weight ensures you have ONE OBJECT and ONE FAULT or VARIANCE that equates to a sound problem statement; see Figure 13.3.

Problem Statement:
Bob's ZEBRA sales are 20% under budget

Figure 13.3 Sample problem statement with specificity relative to product line (i.e., Zebra) and the quantified amount (20%) under the budget goal

2   Clarify variance detail in IS and BUT NOT categories for what, where and when areas

The value of having a process or known set of questions is speed and clarity, as well as not assuming something is fact. This notion of making thinking visible for yourself and those you work with CANNOT be underestimated. The question categories for the IS–BUT NOT format include:

- **WHAT**
- **WHERE**
- **WHEN**

See Figures 13.4 and 13.5 for examples.

3   Generate and destructively test causes

Once the problem statement is described and problem specified, this is when professional grade root-cause tools such as KEPNERandFOURIE CauseWise © separate themselves from others such as the Fishbone Diagram or the 5 WHYs.

Fishbone and 5 WHYs **have no set method to destructively test possible causes** using IS–BUT NOT data.

	Is	But Not
What	1. What is the object you are having a problem with? 2. What is wrong with the object? (Fault)	1. What other similar object(s) could reasonably have the same fault, but does not? 2. What other similar faults could reasonably be observed with the object, but is not?
Where	3. Geographically where is the object when the fault is noticed? 4. Where is the fault located on the object?	3. Where else could the faulty object be observed, but is not? 4. Where else could the fault be located on the object, but is not?
When	5. At which time and date was the fault first noticed? 6. What is the pattern of occurrences? 7. When in the sequence of events of the object was the fault first noticed?	5. When could the fault have been noticed first, but was not? 6. What could the pattern of occurrences be? 7. When else could the fault have been first noticed in the object's sequence of events, but was not?

Figure 13.4 Questions to specify the IS–BUT NOT for any positive or negative problem statement: KEPNERandFOURIE CauseWise © Questions (Copyright 1998 © KEPNERandFOURIE. All rights reserved. V 3.0)

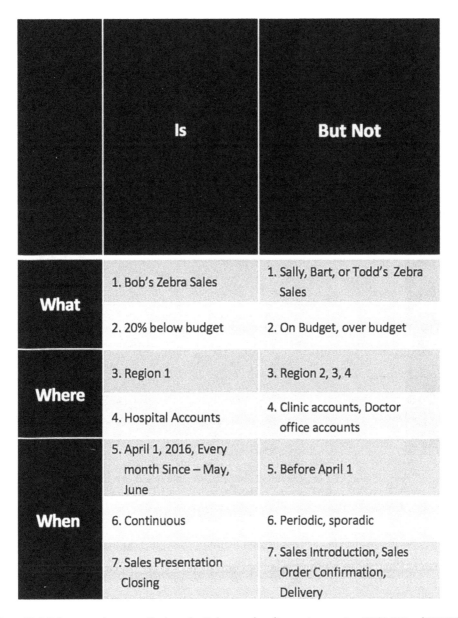

	Is	**But Not**
What	1. Bob's Zebra Sales	1. Sally, Bart, or Todd's Zebra Sales
	2. 20% below budget	2. On Budget, over budget
Where	3. Region 1	3. Region 2, 3, 4
	4. Hospital Accounts	4. Clinic accounts, Doctor office accounts
When	5. April 1, 2016, Every month Since – May, June	5. Before April 1
	6. Continuous	6. Periodic, sporadic
	7. Sales Presentation Closing	7. Sales Introduction, Sales Order Confirmation, Delivery

Figure 13.5 Sales example to specify sheet for Zebra product line variance using KEPNERandFOURIE CauseWise © Questions (Copyright 1998 © KEPNERandFOURIE. All rights reserved. V 3.0)

This missing link can lead to teams assuming they know the cause but really don't. The possible causes (see Figure 13.6) that are generated are subjected to a question that uses both IS-BUT NOT data:

"How does this possible cause (PC) explain both the IS and BUT NOT information?"

	Is	But Not	**Generate and Test __EACH__ Possible Cause (PC1..PCn) against the 7 Pairs of IS-BUT NOT Questions** •Mark A if Assumption required and needs to be validated for the cause to be viable •Mark X if it satisfies IS-BUT NOT Data — meaning it's factual
What	1. Bob's Zebra Sales	1. Sally, Bart, or Todd's Zebra Sales	PC1-Bob is an unmotivated Rep 1 2 3 4 5 6 7
	2. 20% below budget	2. On Budget, over budget	
Where	3. Region 1	3. Region 2, 3, 4	PC2-Competition is too strong 1 2 3 4 5 6 7
	4. Hospital Accounts	4. Clinic accounts, Doctor office accounts	PC3-Bob does not get reports showing his performance
When	5. April 1, 2016, Every month Since – May, June	5. Before April 1	1 2 3 4 5 6 7
	6. Continuous	6. Periodic, sporadic	PC4-Bob did not attend Zebra Sales Closing Skills Training Session
	7. Sales Presentation Closing	7. Sales Introduction, Sales Order Confirmation, Delivery	1 2 3 4 5 6 7

Figure 13.6 First GENERATE possible causes for Zebra sales performance under performing using IS-BUT NOT comparison data. KEPNERandFOURIE CauseWise © Questions (Copyright 1998 © KEPNERandFOURIE. All rights reserved. V 3.0)

This question acts as filter to give each possible cause a fair shot at being the root cause and ensures the team is using FACTUAL data. Causes that can't explain the IS-BUT NOT data are eliminated and noted, and the reasons why and/or assumptions made to "make the cause viable" are noted.

It's important to note at this point that you may not always reach the final cause in the first pass. But if your team started with eight possible causes for a given profit decline, and you have eliminated four through sound questioning, you have divided your goose chase in half – **you now have double the scarce resources dedicated to finding the real cause.**

4   *Confirm assumptions to find root cause*

As with any problem-solving and decision-making, many times you must make a number of assumptions that you will need to confirm, qualify or disprove through a robust process as the final step before taking action. Using a consistent process for root cause again forces your executive team of practitioners to lead with data (see Figure 13.7).

In summary, we started this chapter with the most important graphic I have ever seen high-performance executives use. This positive and negative variance assessment on your three strategic goals, the cells in your PMC Engine and your Strategic Performance Indicators sets up your team to use its strategy, make mid-course corrections and source data to drive decisions, as outlined in Figure 13.8.

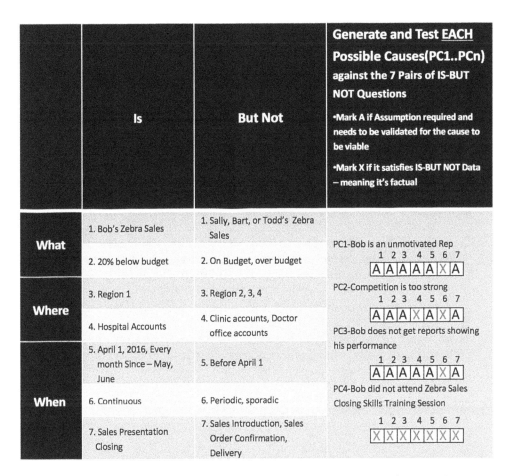

Figure 13.7 Full Zebra root cause example. This example clearly shows possible causes (PC1, PC2, PC3) that – to be true – have many assumptions that need to be validated versus the PC4 cause that explains both the IS and BUT NOT data for each 7 Pairs of questions denoted with the "X." PC4 is factually based and is the most likely cause of the performance gap; more specific action can now be taken and, importantly, wild goose chases can be avoided. KEPNERandFOURIE CauseWise © Questions (Copyright 1998 © KEPNERandFOURIE. All rights reserved. V 3.0).

Scrutinize (+) and (-) variances in your:

- 3 Strategic Goals
- PMC Product-Market Cells
- Strategic Performance Indicators

Use a Robust Root Cause Analysis Process.
You will uncover missed opportunities

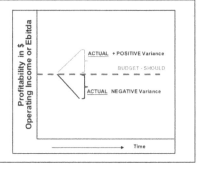

Figure 13.8 The most powerful graphic ever! SHOULD versus ACTUAL performance graph

 Now what

At the end of the day, the strategy system and tools come down to making the performance of your business visible so you can manage the positive and negative deviations and take action. To enable and equip your team to find cause, start by getting back to these simple actions:

1   Commit the team to the expectation that using the tools is to deliver results and sustainable profitability – not to showcase the tools
2   Select a common process for problem-solving – and it really should be something more than the 5 WHYs; the 5 WHYs is a good starting point to state a problem, but not effective detail to determine cause in most cases
3   Recognize that the WHY behind positive and negative variances in business is really what many management leadership team meetings should be based on.

14 Check in quarterly

Use it or lose it

 After 5pm

If your quarterly review sessions have turned into static presentations, now is the time to change that. Five guidelines are laid out that will make your quarterly and yearly strategic reviews effective and productive.

Quarterly reviews are critical to surface issues that impede or exploit strategic progress against your three strategic goals.

Using your strategy system tools – Strategic Assumptions, PMC Engine and SPIs – to collaboratively addresses issues is best accomplished with a consistent Checkpoint structure to embed the behavior that strategy is a process, not an event.

Even in volatile times, you and your competitors are facing the same economic and environment factors. Global events do not single out only your company.

To equip your firm to proactively respond to external and internal issues (rather than react), you should be able to clearly answer these questions; if you can't, then there are solutions in this chapter to improve how you can embed and use your strategy to drive results. The questions are:

- **How much time do you and your executives spend quarterly using and testing your strategy to make mid-course corrections?**
- **Do you have a set quarterly meeting format to drive strategy meetings?**
- **Is there a mechanism you have to collect and move strategic issues up to the leadership table?**
- **Can your executive team distinguish between strategic versus operational issues?**
- **How do you build Market and Competitive Intelligence into your strategy process or cycle?**

The best-performing companies and most-compelling CEOs we work with can answer these questions and have built a smart review system to check their strategies.

Companies that grow profitably during certain and uncertain times do so by using their strategy to test alignment and competitiveness of their organization against the backdrop of relevant global issues impacting performance.

They are masters at being able to strategically sort relevant from the irrelevant and make mid-course corrections with the help of their TDG Strategy System tools to ensure sustained value creation (EBITDA growth).

Making strategy work – quarterly checkpoints based on five principles

You need to review strategy checkpoints on a quarterly basis – monthly is usually too operational and yearly is too distant to be meaningful. To have an effective strategic cadence that respects **working in and working on** the business, the following principles or guidelines are recommended:

Guideline 1: the purpose is to resolve issues not present data

All executives can read.

Most executives are tired of either preparing decks of slides or presenting them to their peers. And most of their leadership team peers don't want to sit through their presentations. Many of them have already seen or talked about the data in an afterhours call or hallway conversation – so why have a quarterly review that regurgitates this information?

The CEO pays top executives to solve problems and make decisions, not sit through presentations. If presenting data is all your quarterly reviews do, then you are wasting time and money.

Second, while there are some presentation slides that may be needed, there should be a pack of slides that go to the executive team a week before you hold the meeting. Their job is to review and reflect on what the data is saying and find or be prepared to find the causes for those areas of over and under performance relative to the three strategic goals, variances in the PMC Engine cells and SPIs that they discover.

Quarterly Reviews (QRs) need to isolate and identify one or two issues that require executive experience, expertise and cross-functional viewpoints to resolve them. Any QR should be about working together to resolve these issues, not presenting bar and line charts.

Guideline 2: timing and purpose of Quarterly Reviews

Quarterly meetings should be set at least once per quarter – at a time when the latest financial information is available. In addition, QRs should run prior to board meetings, as this gives the team time to come to grips with positive or negative variations in performance before fielding board questions.

Three of the Quarterly Reviews by a leadership team are generally focused on resolving performance issues and one of them, during the mid-year, is reserved to dig deeper into their next-generation strategy if required. The key takeaway when setting up Quarterly Reviews is to make sure the intent and objectives are thought through ahead of time and made visual.

The one (or at least one of) the gripes I hear from CEOs I work with is the over-abundance of meetings and calls that seem to be happening with their executive teams. One CEO told me he was having trouble scheduling time with his own team to discuss strategic issues. This seems to be more the norm that the exception from my experience.

The point of sharing this is that, for a company to actually use their strategy and tools they will develop from this book, they have to create a set structure and purpose for their strategy team to work within.

Many companies have not sat back and thought through why they have certain activities occurring during the year that consume mammoth amounts of resources but with diminishing returns.

As discussed earlier, budgets, strategy and LRPs can each take on a life of their own in companies whereas leaders could simplify redundancies by using the PMC Engine as the basis for all.

To help you begin to think about the purpose and format for your QRs and annual planning requirements (see Figures 14.1–14.3), I have included three examples/templates to:

1   Create a simple annual calendar that you can refine and make yours
2   Integrate a tried-and-true agenda for holding effective QRs
3   Follow a format for objectives and roles/responsibilities in QRs.

Guideline 3: SHOULD versus ACTUAL – finding the why behind positive and negative deviations using strategic goals, PMC Engine and SPIs

The TDG Strategy System – Assumptions, PMC Engine and SPIs – all work together to set up signals for how your business is performing relative to targets that were set. Put another way, is the ACTUAL achieving the SHOULD? These tools are your three one-page control centers to drive decisions and mid-course corrections from.

Sample Schedule for Quarterly Strategy Reviews and Board Meetings											
Meeting	JAN	FEB	MAR	APR	MAY	JUN	JUL	AUG	SEP	OCT	NOV	DEC
QRs			QR 1			QR 2			QR 3			QR4
QR Purpose			Performance Review using PMC Engine and SPIs			Performance Review using PMC Engine and SPIs			Performance Review using PMC Engine and SPIs			Performance Review, PMC BUDGET Finalization
BOARD	BD1			BD2			BD3			BD4		
BOARD Purpose	Strategic update and Financial Performance			Strategic update and Financial Performance			Strategic update and Financial Performance			Strategic update on Next year and Financial Forecast		

Figure 14.1 Quarterly strategy review and board meeting sample schedule

600am

1. Status Last Meeting Open Action Items –

Where necessary for ELT alignment/closure

630am

2. Review SPI Variances +/ –

Focus on variances, understand root cause and actions required
May require reference to PMC ENGINE and other established tools

730am

3. Implementation: Key Projects Status/Issues

A. Projects – Q and Implementation Initiatives 1-5

B. Q4 E-survey Results

BREAK – 15 minutes--

900am

4. New Strategic Issues for ELT Discussion

① **Review SA issues "consolidated" from Q4 SA's conducted across the organization**

② **ELT to appraise and agree to the most serious, urgent and growing issues for FY2012 and determine how the existing strategy and implementation plans align to address them**

245pm

5. Closeout, Communication and Action items

Figure 14.2 Agenda and structure for a Quarterly Review meeting

In the context of a QR meeting, every participating team member should come prepared with the following information and understand how the tools link together to ask and answer performance questions:

A Strategic Assumptions

Assumptions are the foundation of the strategy. We need to check to see if our assumptions are unfolding as we expected and at a rate of change we forecasted.

Similarly, do our Product, Market and Capability decisions defined in our Implications still make sense? Meaning, do they remain the best options to exploit or mitigate trends we foresaw?

Depending on the answers to these questions, is there an opportunity to make corrections and speed up, slow down or apportion resources to those areas required by the strategy (most likely associated with initiatives derived from key Capabilities)?

1. Meeting Objectives

1. Appraise Business Performance and Gaps to Date

*   Assess Business and Implementation Progress to Targets – Focus on gaps, +/-variances, and actions required to resolve

2. Identify Issues Requiring ELT Input and Involvement to Resolve

*   Ensure issues are separated and clarified, discussed and understood and solutions to resolve issue are agreed upon

3. Determine Action and Responsibility

*   Ensure clear action and responsibility for interim analysis, evaluation and solution generation are agreed upon and have one person accountable

2. Roles and Responsibilities

Strategy Coordinator

*   Send out pre-meeting information and assignments as required for the ELT to effectively prepare for the issues to be addressed – consolidate and communicate outcomes

Facilitator - CEO or selected ELT member or Outsider

*   Lead the meeting, ensure issues are kept at appropriate level to ensure clarity, alignment and clear activities arise from the session. Cultivate healthy discourse

Participants – ELT

*   Assist team to focus on meaningful progress to date, barriers that need to be addressed and solutions to be implemented.
*   Ensure preparation for areas you will be discussing with team and engage/challenge others to cultivate understanding and alignment on issues

Figure 14.3 Quarterly Review meeting objectives and roles

In practice, Assumptions don't usually change in mid-course of a strategy, but the rates of change (e.g., growth rates of markets and/or competitive response) become clearer and the team has more confidence in where to deploy resources.

B Strategic Performance Indicators (SPIs)
We defined SPIs as the eight indicators (four LEADING and four LAGGING) that define the health of your strategy and financial performance. During a QR session,

each of these should be evaluated on ACTUAL versus SHOULD performance, with the team evaluating possible causes of positive and negative variances.

C   Three Strategic Goals
Strategic goals were encapsulated in the SPIs but are an important subset; the team must evaluate ACTUAL versus SHOULD performance. These three goals were the ones that defined success for the organization in a calendar year and rose above all else.

D   PMC Engine
As discussed throughout this book, the PMC Engine is the decision-making hub that sets relative priority for each Product-Market cell. During QRs, it provides the next "double click down" of detail to understand what is working and not working in the strategy. So rather than generalizing about consolidated results – be they over or under budget – we now use the PMC Engine to evaluate which Product-Market Cells have variances, find cause and take the appropriate team actions.

These four tools can and should be used by the CEO and executive as the performance dashboard to run their business and strategically drive the company forward. The summary of the TDG Strategy System in Figure 14.4 helps executives use their strategy throughout the year to determine status and make corrections.

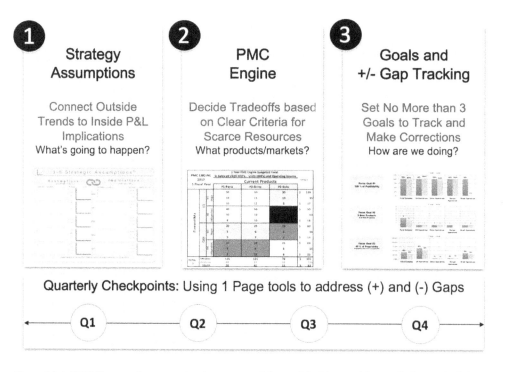

Figure 14.4 TDG Strategy System: a simple yet powerful set of decision-making tools that embed decision and finding root cause

Guideline 4: issues blocking the achievement of your strategic
goals should come from the organization, not just the executive team

In many companies, QRs tend to run late or be detail bound and complex. Often this is because no one wants to "miss anything" or "fail to respond" to critical strategic issues. Having attended and participated in many such meetings, I see the cause of such meetings attributed to four main reasons:

- **Teams zero in on interesting but irrelevant information.**
- **No method is used to quickly sort strategic and operational issues.**
- **No context for the type of issues is provided – is this a problem, a decision or a risk? (That is, is this concerning the past, present or future context?)**
- **They have no common executive toolbox to find cause, make decisions or assess risk.**

To counter these pitfalls and make your QRs (or any executive meeting) more productive and outcome based, you can employ the **QR Issue Assessment Tool** shown in Figure 14.5. It helps executives source, sort and frame issues more effectively – and in a common format.

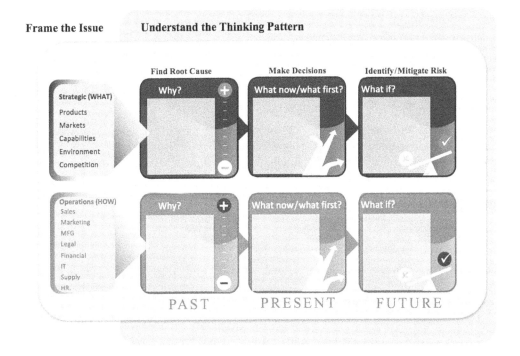

Figure 14.5 QR Issue Assessment Tool: use this framework to gather and sort relevant issues so your team understands the type of issue and the pattern of thinking that's required

This simple issue-gathering tool will:

- **Speed your assessment** of any situation because it is repeatable and captures all the issues
- **Reinforce your confidence** that a complete view of the situation has been captured
- **Provide content guidance** as to what type of issue you are dealing with
- Encourage you to **separate strategic from operational issues**
- **Make issues visible** so your people can easily collaborate
- **Quietly teach the difference between strategy and operational thinking**

Guideline 5: feed relevant marketing intelligence to QRs

Your people need **relevant external data** to make timely and actionable decisions relative to their products and markets in order to maximize profits. If you do not generate contextual, external data, you will be making decisions in a vacuum.

There are actually three truisms when it comes to Market Intelligence – actionable data that results in stronger strategic decisions. All of these describe things that are within your control.

A   No company has perfect data about the competition, customer and environment

Regardless of your industry, your company size or the location of your business, there is no utopian Market Intelligence report or system that will give you all the answers or perfect information. Removing this "the earth is flat" idea from your company is a secret to enabling better Market Intelligence. If you have ever purchased an industry report, most likely the data has come from your people who have been interviewed by the report consolidator. This leads me to the next point.

B   The best Market Intelligence comes from your people

The source of this content is their current relationships with customers, suppliers, competitors and government officials. Many executives find this hard to believe, but the truth is your employees offer current and timely insight that will drive better decision-making only if they are being asked the right questions and being guided in a way to consolidate the data to make it actionable to those who need it to make better decisions (decisions that impact Products, Market and Capabilities).

C   The system to gather and consolidate data must be simple

If the system is not simple, your people will not collect the information or use it. While I support technology as an enabler to decision-making, I am blown away by the time and money spent on "software systems" that go unused or unpopulated by many companies.

The best intelligence is relevant questions the company develops against the backdrop of the PMC Engine.

Why the PMC Engine? Because it is the single-page decision-making hub developed to allocate scarce resources, and those decisions need to be examined against an additional filter of external data.

Key questions that form the starting point for sound Market Intelligence and that the best companies ask and know the answers for include:

1 What is the $ size of this Product-Market cell?
2 What is the per cent growth over your time frame?
3 What is your market share in $ and units?
4 Who are the key competitors?
5 What are their current strengths/competitive advantages?
6 What weighted criteria drive customer purchase decisions?
7 Who could be a key competitor?
8 Why would they enter this product/market space?

Answering these questions using the PMC Engine as a construct or backdrop offers the following immediate benefits:

1 **PRIORITY**
   The relative priority is immediate because Product-Market cells have colors that represent your team's thinking on the HIGH, MEDIUM and LOW emphasis.
2 **DATA GAPS**
   Data gaps force you to confront what holes you have in the Product-Market cell you compete in and what actions you can take to close them.
3 **OUTSIDE-to-IN VIEW**
   When resolving issues on specific Product-Market situations, your team must consider the EXTERNAL factors of the world, which is data that is critical to set the context of the decision.
4 **COMMON COMPANY VIEW**
   The Market Intelligence captured with the PMC Engine overlay allows the full team to have a single view of the industry they compete in. In addition, the team can delegate this task to junior and/or new employees to quickly get them up to speed on the market.
5 **CUSTOMER BUYING CRITERIA**
   This format forces teams to confront how well customer purchase criteria are known (or not). Additionally, this intelligence tool tests how effectively your competitive positioning is working.
   For example if your team espouses that you focus on niche markets and get a PRICE PREMIUM relative to the competition but notes in the matrix that PRICE is the key driver of buying decisions, this alerts you to a misalignment on thinking, data quality and positioning – or some combination of all of this.

When these questions are answered and put together in a decision-making tool, this Market Intelligence Matrix (MIM) becomes an integral part of the QR and ongoing data collection process for making better decisions and spotting changes in the marketplace.

In the sample MIM shown in Figure 14.6, one cell has been completed for illustration purposes only. In practice when working with clients, they complete each cell and find that they are able to find patterns in data more readily, assess the source and level of confidence they have in the data, and customize it by adding their own questions.

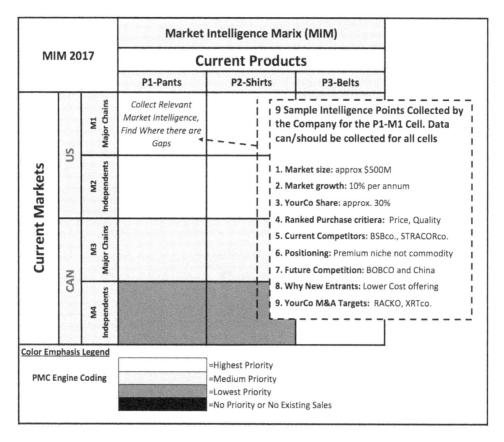

Figure 14.6 MIM sample: one cell completed for illustration purpose – in practice all cells with resources directed at them are completed. This relative High, Medium and Low emphasis, as represented by the PMC Engine color coding, should be used again to prioritize what data collection should be a priority.

With the MIM being deployed and available to executives and functional leaders in the company, the organization begins to align and channel the vast levels of expertise for making better decisions.

Now what

Tools don't create results – people do. Meetings don't create results – the right people with the right information do. The tools outlined in this chapter and book will not make your business better unless you put them to use and recognize that iterations in understanding and application are needed.

This chapter outlines five guidelines and supporting tools or examples for you to effectively use your strategy to **MAKE BIG DECISIONS BETTER**. Recognize that it takes sweat equity to learn, embed and use the tools, but they become your own.

This ownership is fortified by ensuring you and your team:

1   Resolve rather than present issues
2   Set structure and purpose in a schedule that promotes use of the tools
3   Focus on the WHY in the suite of simple tools this system builds
4   Set context for finding the issues that are blocking your strategy
5   Make decisions from an outside-to-in perspective using the MIM as that external filter.

The last word on decision-making goes to Chuck Kepner, our founder who passed away in 2016 and always kept things practical, simple and relevant for our clients.

"The sum total of daily decisions made by your people determines the fate of your organization."

Dr. Chuck Kepner

Index